ALLIED UNITS OF WORLD WA

THE 1st (US) INFANTRY DIVISION

Stéphane LAVIT and
Philippe CHARBONNIER

Sophia Histoire & Collections

Preface

Today, the 1st Infantry Division is the oldest regular division of the United States Army. Activated in 1917, it was the first to set foot in France, where it would go on to acquire its fine reputation. During the Second World War, where it was led by hard-headed and born leaders of men, such as General Terry Allen, it was the first American division to be based in England. It was also amongst the first to fight against Axis forces in North Africa. Following the hard fighting in Sicily, where its prowess endowed it with a feeling of superiority, the 'Big Red One' was selected for another tough mission, the invasion of Normandy. It then went on to be the first to set foot on German soil after crossing the Rhine. After 1945, the 1st Infantry Division played a vital role in the Cold War in Europe, before being deployed in Vietnam. At the end of the 20th Century, the Division found itself based in Germany, then the Balkans and the Gulf. In more recent times, its units have been regularly deployed in Iraq and Afghanistan.

Stéphane Lavit & Philippe Charbonnier

Contents

1 - Birth of a division

Motto of the 1st Infantry Division: "No Mission Too Difficult, No Sacrifice Too Great - Duty First"

This photo was taken during the Spanish-American War of 1898. It shows troops of the 16th Infantry in trenches near Santiago de Cuba.

Above. A 16th Infantry soldier armed with the Krag-Jorgensen rifle, circa 1898.

Right. A young 16th Infantry soldier in the Philippines, 1914.

The 1st Infantry Division of the United States Army has had a rich history since its organization in 1917. However, some of its component units are older and are steeped in tradition.

The 16th Infantry (Regiment) is a regular army unit that was created in 1798. It saw action against the British in the War of 1812, then against Mexico, then in the Civil War, then against Native Americans and in the Philippines. At the beginning of the 20th Century, it was part of the punitive expedition in Mexico before being called upon to take part in the First World War.

The 18th Infantry was created during the War of 1812. On 4 May 1861, it was tasked with ensuring the safety of President Lincoln and was then reorganized during the Civil War which, once ended, saw them fighting the Native Americans during the period of colonization, as well as along the borders. In the Philippines, it marched against the Moro rebels before taking part in the war of 1898 against Spain in Cuba.

The 26th Infantry arrived in Manila on 18 March 1901 in order to fight the Philippine rebels. The regiment was called back to the United States in July 1903 to guard the Mexican border. Between May 1907 and June 1909, the unit served in the Philippines. It then saw garrison duty in Michigan until 1913 before heading for Texas in order to patrol the Mexican border.

The war in Europe

The 1st Expeditionary Division, created on 24 May 1917, began its organization the following 8 June at Fort Jay (New York) under the command of Brigadier General William L. Sibert. It was the first division created in order to fight German forces in Europe. It comprised of four infantry regiments, three artillery regiments and was completed by supporting units. In all, the Division comprised of almost 28,000 men.

Men of the 16th Infantry marching near the Mexican border during the punitive expedition against Pancho Villa in March 1916.

THE BIG RED ONE

In France, the division earned its nickname of "Big red One" as a reference to its shoulder patch, a non-regulation badge that appeared late in the war.
Its origins remain uncertain. The first version has it that the trucks issued to the division were British and in order to differentiate them from other Allied materiel, the drivers painted large numerals "1" on the sides.
The shoulder patch, in its original form, was a large red 1 cut from the band of captured German soldiers' caps.
It was approved on 31 October by HQ/ American Expeditionary Force (AEF).

The 1st Division Honor Guard before parading in Paris on 4 July 1917, Independence Day. This parade was carried out to boost French morale.

In France

The Division's first units embarked in the ports of New York and Hoboken (New Jersey) on 14 June 1917. They landed at Saint-Nazaire and Liverpool a week later. Captain George Marshall, the future Chief of Staff of the United States Army, was the second officer in the division to set foot in France. After a short period of additional training, the Doughboys were sent to France at last. The Division's last units arrived from the United States on 22 December 1917. In France, the infantry was grouped together at Gondrecourt le Château (Meuse). As for the divisional artillery, it was sent to a camp at Valdahon in the Doubs department. The unit became the 1st Division and, on 4 July 1917, the American Independence Day, the 2nd Battalion, 16th Infantry, paraded in the streets of Paris. On 8 August, the Division adopted the Square table of organization comprising of two infantry brigades, one of engineers, a signals battalion, three machine-gun battalions, a three-regiment artillery brigade and supply train. The total strength now reached 27,120 officers and men. On the morning of 23 Oc-

August 1917. The Doughboys of the 1st Division spent their first months in France at Gondrecourt le Château where they were trained in trench warfare by a French Chasseurs battalion. (National Archives via J. Gawne)

Gondrecourt le Château. Men undergo training with the Hotchkiss machine-gun. As was the also the case with artillery, automatic weapons were supplied by the French and British allies. (National Archives via J. Gawne)

Below. March 1918 in the Toul sector. This soldier of the 5th Field Artillery has just finished queuing for chow; his rations also include cigarettes. (National Archives via J. Gawne)

tober 1917, the first American shells fell on German positions in the Toul Sector of Eastern France. Two days later, the 2/16th Infantry incurred its first losses. In December, the Division was placed under the command of Major-General Robert Lee Bullard. In March 1918, the Germans launched the Ludendorff offensives. In May, the army group commanded by the Kronprinz broke through the French Aisne sector and advanced as far as Château-Thierry, 64 kms north-east of Paris. The 1st Division was sent to Picardy to assist the 1st French army to stabilize the front. The 1st Division faced the village of Cantigny, built on top of a hill surrounded by woods. The 28th Infantry attacked the village and captured it after 45 minutes of hard fighting, at the terrible cost of 1,067 killed and wounded.

The Doughboys, who had taken a hundred prisoners, had achieved the first American victory of the war. The men of the 28th Infantry

Bottom left. A postcard showing the battle honours of the 1st Division in 1917-1918.

First American Troops to Land in France and last to go home

FIRST
in sector.
to shoot at Germans.
to attack.
to conduct a raid.
to be raided.
to capture prisoners.
to suffer casualties.
to be cited singly in general orders.
in number of division, corps and Army Commanders and General Staff Officers produced from its personnel.

In front line 220 days.
Captured 163 officers and 6,304 men, 119 pieces of field artillery, 62 trench mortars, 413 machine guns.
Casualties 21,612.
Killed and died of wounds 4,411.
Replacements received 30,206.
Distinguished service crosses won 356.

Below. Seen here at the Division's homecoming parade in Washington, this 28th Infantry truck bears the names of the battles in which the Regiment took part in France. (National Archives via J. Gawne)

became known as the "Black Lions of Cantigny". Soissons was liberated by the Division in July 1918 but losses were heavy: 700 killed, wounded and missing. From 11-13 September, the Doughboys helped the French pinch off the Saint-Mihiel Salient and were then involved in their final battles in the Meuse-Argonne forest where they advanced seven kilometers. The total casualties of the 1st Division during the First World War were 4,411 killed, 17,201 wounded and 1,056 missing.

The inter-war period

In September 1919, the 1st Division returned to the United States where it stood down from its war footing at Camp Zachary Taylor, Kentucky. It then returned to New York and set up its headquarters at Fort Hamilton (Brooklyn). It was one of the three regular army divisions to be retained in peacetime, the rest of the AEF divisions having been inactivated. It underwent further restructuring on 7 October 1920: two infantry brigades, one artillery brigade, one medical unit and the divisional supply train. Its total strength stood at 19,385 men.

Right. General Holbrook, commander of the 1st Division engineers, seen here in the 1930s observing his men crossing the Delaware river at the same point where George Washington crossed in 1777.

Below. This 1919 poster asks men to enlist in one of the regular divisions, one of which was the 1st Division.

Below. Just before the Second World War, the American doctrine was still unsure as to whether use tanks in an infantry support role or as part of an independent mobile force. This photo, dated 23 August 1939, shows light tanks of the 1st Tank Company at Plattsburgh Barracks, New York State, demonstrating tactics with men of the 26th Infantry.

2 - Stateside Training

1st Division machine-gunners training at one of New York harbor's forts (skyscrapers can be seen in the distance) in 1936.

Right insert. The distinctive insignia of the divisional headquarters, adopted on 8 September. Red and blue are the colors of infantry divisions, the victory figure is that of the division's memorial in Washington DC.

Below. A Dodge VC-5 truck belonging to the 16th Infantry and armed with a heavy machine-gun in an anti-aircraft position, seen here during the 3rd Army maneuvers at Fort Benning, Georgia, April 1940.

Bottom right. On this April 1940-dated aerial photo, soldiers of the Division form the "Big Red One" at Fort Benning.

In September 1939, the 1st Division adopted a new table of organization and equipment. The new, easier to handle 'triangular' division, included three infantry regiments.

During the emergency period decreed by President Roosevelt before the country was plunged into war, there was a huge intake of recruits. Seen here in 1939, these draftees are being clothed upon their induction into the 1st Division.

Below. Each soldier was also issued with a 'footlocker' for storing equipment and personal items. This one has been packed according to regulations and is placed in front of the bed for inspection.

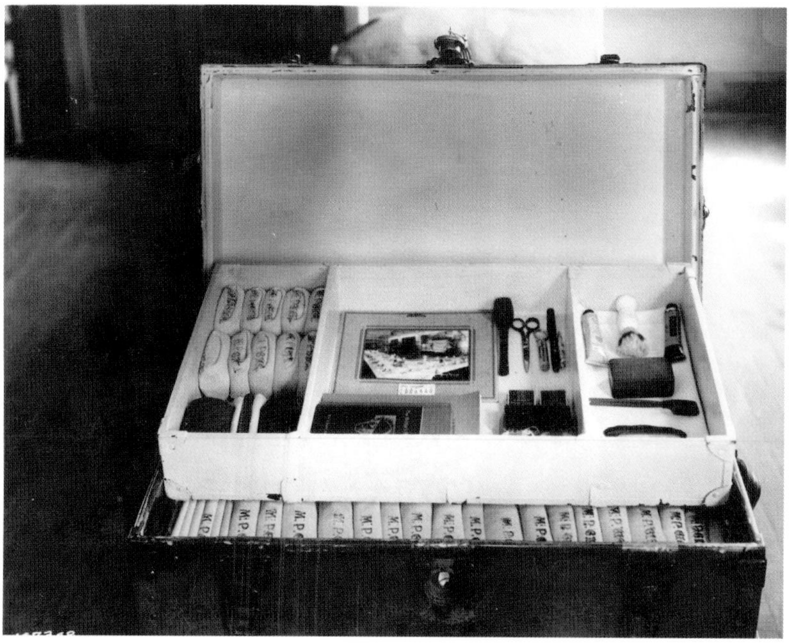

The total strength now stood at 9,057 officers and men. The Division moved to Fort Benning (Georgia) on 19 November 1939 then left for large-scale maneuvers in Louisiana on 11 May 1940.

It returned to Fort Hamilton (Brooklyn) on 5 June. Garrisoned at Fort Devens (Massachusetts) from February 1941, The Division took part in maneuvers in the two Carolina states in October and November before returning to Fort Devens on 6 December 1941. The following day, the Japanese fleet launched a surprise attack against the naval base at Pearl Harbor in Hawaii. President Roosevelt subsequently declared war on the Japanese empire. On 12 December, Germany and Italy declared war on the United States as stipulated by the Tripartite Pact. During the winter of 1941, the Big Red One underwent intensive amphibious training and moved to Camp Blanding, in Florida, on 21 February 1942. On 15 May 1942, and with a strength of 15,000 men, it was renamed the 1st Infantry Division (in order to distinguish it from the 1st Armored Division).

It returned to Fort Benning on 22 May, then moved towards the large training ground at the Indiantown Gap Military Reservation in Penn-

Right.
Soldiers of the 16th Infantry training at Fort Devens (Massachusetts) in 1941.

sylvania from 21 June onwards. The Big Red One next received orders to prepare for overseas deployment. Its units embarked in the port of New York on 1 August 1942. The convoy set sail the following day and crossed the Atlantic without an escort. The bulk of the Division was on board the famous liner, the *Queen Mary*. The convoy reached Scotland on 7 August and the Division went to Tidworth Barracks in England in order to continue its amphibious assault training. On 16 October, the entire division boarded ships again, this time for its baptism of fire. Indeed, on the 26th, the convoy set sail for North Africa; Operation Torch had begun.

Far right.
August 1941, the 1st Infantry Division on amphibious maneuvers in the New River sector, North Carolina. An NCO points out a target to a Browning Automatic Rifle (BAR) team. The mosquito nets on the helmets were a necessity.

Below.
4 June 1941 at Buzzard Bay, men of the 16th Infantry during a landing exercise on the Massachusetts coast. The men are jumping off launches that are ill-suited to the rapid discharge of troops on shore.

A 16th Infantry rifle squad moving off the beach during an amphibious assault exercise at New River. The wear the pre-war blue denim fatigue clothing.

Below.
The regiment's GIs clamber down the netting hanging along the hull of the troop ship USS Wakefield during an exercise for transferring men into landing craft.

Below right.
Field Marshal Sir John Dill, the British military representative in Washington at the Joint Chiefs of Staff, watches men of the 16th Infantry during his visit to Camp Blanding on 1 May 1942.

The following photographs were taken during the large-scale maneuvers in Louisiana in May 1940. We first see short-barrel 155mm howitzers lined up in a bivouac area.

Right.
A convoy of 16th Infantry light trucks drives through a town as the Division heads towards the maneuvers zone.

Above.
A sergeant is attaching a sign for the divisional HQ to a tree.

Below. Filtering and filling large drinking water containers at the Company H, 18th Infantry Regiment camp.

Above.
A GI grabs a quick rest from pitching tents. His garrison cap is a left-over from 1918 stocks.

Below.
At the HQ battery of a field artillery battalion. The men still wear the felt Campaign hat that pre-dates the Great War.

3 - North Africa

"Nothing in hell can stop the 1st Division"

Right. 12 November 1942, 26th Infantry officers on board the British troop ship Monarch of Bermuda. Note the flags on the sleeve and the round tactical insignia on the map case of the man on the left.

Below. On 26 October 1942, the Division left Scotland by ship and headed towards Morocco. Some of the 16th Infantry and its equipment were transported on the troopship HMT Warwick Castle.

At the end of 1942, the Allies attempted a large-scale landing in North Africa in order to take the pressure off the British army in Libya.

These forces attacked the coastline from Morocco to Algeria that were defended by Vichy French troops. The 1st Division was under the command of Major General Terry de la Mesa Allen, and his second in command was Brigadier General Theodore Roosevelt, Jr. Accompanied by a Combat Command of the 1st Armored and by the 1st Ranger Battalion, it made up the Center Task Force, whose task was to capture the port of Oran, defended by more than fifty coastal artillery pieces and numerous fortifications. After having spent several months in England, the soldiers of the Big Red One landed on the Algerian coast: the 16th and 18th Infantry to the east of Oran and the 26th Infantry at Les Andalouses to the west. The 18th Infantry quickly moved off the seaside and headed towards Saint-Cloud where it was halted by fierce resistance. As for the 16th Infantry, they were pinned down in front of La Macta. The 26th Infantry was busy knocking out coastal positions, including the fort of Aïn el Turk that was holding out. Due to a lack of vehicles, the infantry advance could not be speeded up and preparations were made for coordinated action the following day. On 9 November, the 18th Infantry was once more halted at Saint-Cloud, firmly held by the French. Finally, General Allen decided to go around the village rather than pulverize it with

The 16th Infantry landed at Arzew at dawn on 8 November 1942.

Above and below.
The 26th Infantry landed on the beach at Les Andalouses west of Oran.

ORDER OF BATTLE OF THE 1st INFANTRY DIVISION, 1942-45

16th Infantry Regiment
18th Infantry Regiment
26th Infantry Regiment

Divisional Artillery:
5th Field artillery Battalion (155 mm)
7th Field artillery Battalion (105 mm)
32nd Field artillery Battalion (105 mm)
33rd Field artillery Battalion (105 mm)

1st Reconnaissance Troop. Mecz
1st Engineer Combat Battalion
1st Medical Battalion
1st Counter Intelligence Corps Detachment
Headquarters Special Troops
Hqs Company, 1st Infantry Division
701st Ordnance Light Maintenance Company
1st Quartermaster Company
1st Signal Company
Military Police Platoon

artillery and risk hitting the civilians still present there. On the left flank, the 16th Infantry was still held in check by the defenses at La Macta. The French launched a counter-attack in the morning from Mostaganem and, for a while, posed a threat to the foremost American elements. At Aïn el Turk, the 26th Infantry obtained the surrender of the forts at Cap Faucon. However, during the night, its rear area was threatened by French infiltration. On the morning of 10 November and under pressure from General Fredendall (2nd Army Corps), General Allen gave orders to capture Oran as quickly as possible. He ended his order with

The photos on this page illustrate the 2nd Battalion, 16th Infantry marching through Kasserine Pass, towards the east and Feriana on 26 February 1943.

Above. Pte. John F. Plichta, 2nd Battalion, 16th Infantry, moves towards the front line via the Kasserine Pass. He is carrying a 60mm mortar. Plichta, later promoted to staff sergeant, was killed in action on Omaha Beach on 6 June 1944.

the famous words "*Nothing in hell can stop the 1st Division*". Having straightened out its lines and dealt with the threat to its rear, the Division quickly advanced and by around 8am had reached the town's suburbs. As one can read in the Division's history, *Danger Forward*: *"the town of Oran fell without any trouble. When the tanks and lines of infantry marched through the town the streets were lined with civilians. Some were perhaps hostile towards the victors but overall, the population seemed friendly."* The Division then set up tented camps around the town in cold and wet weather.

The Division's men were now veterans, they had undergone their baptism of fire and had lost comrades. The 1st Division was an assault

An aerial view of the Kasserine Pass sector.

division that had lived up to its name. As Teddy Roosevelt said, it would always be ready to march towards the sound of the guns.

In Tunisia

With Montgomery's 8th Army pushing the 'Panzerarmee Afrika' back towards northern Tunisia, the Allies advanced from Algeria with their relatively weak force in order to capture Bizerte and Tunis and finish off the encirclement of the enemy. In the dash from the east, the 1st Division was split up and its units committed piecemeal during the course of ill-planned operations under British command. On 25 November, the 3/26th Infantry was transported by plane towards Youks les Bains and established as a guard opposite the Atlas mountains. The 5th Field Artillery was attached to the British Vth Corps which had also in its ranks an American armor combat command. The 5th fought with distinction but lost its commander and several battery commanders killed in action. It only returned to the Division on 7 February 1943. At the end of November, the 18th Infantry, also attached to Vth Corps, made its way to Tunisia by truck and saw bitter fighting at Longstop Hill and Medjez el Bab. Hitler, even as his armies were on the brink of suffering a catastrophic defeat at Stalingrad, stubbornly kept sending troops and equipment to North Africa. Despite the advance of the British 8th Army in southern Tunisia, he was determined to defeat the Allies in North Africa in order to weaken the coalition and, above all, demoralize the American soldiers in their first taste of combat.

In January, the rest of the 26th Infantry and the 33rd Field Artillery went to the US II Corps south of the country. Along with the 1st Armored Division, they reinforced the French XIX corps. II Corps was deployed piecemeal in central Tunisia and could only advance in order to position itself between von Arnim's 5. Panzer-Armee in the north and Rommel's forces in the south. Eisenhower had planned to hold the passes through the eastern dorsal high ground in Tunisia and set up a strong logistical base at Tebessa in order to launch a large-scale offensive as soon as the rainy season ended in March.

Below. Generals Roosevelt Jr., Allen and Patton observe their troop movements at El Guettar, March 1943. This was the first battle won by the American Army against German forces.

Kasserine

However, as early as mid-February, von Arnim was the first to strike at Faïd Pass and pushed back the French. The 1st Division was ordered to position a regiment at the exit of the pass whilst the 1st Armored deployed in the valley where the road extended from the pass. Coming up against two panzer divisions, the 1st Armored lost half of its tanks at Sidi-Bou-Zid. But the Americans withdrew in an orderly fashion towards Sbeitla. As for Rommel, he gathered a fighting force the size of a division and slipped towards Kasserine Pass on the western dorsal. His objective was, of course, Tebessa and its huge dumps of gas and supplies. Kasserine Pass is, in fact, a narrow passage, less than two kilometers in length, along the floor of a valley. The sector was held by the 26th Infantry, a battalion of the 19th Engineers, a battalion of Tank destroyers, five tanks, two 105 batteries and around a hundred British troops armed with a few light tanks and anti-tank guns. On 20 February, an enemy artillery barrage fell and Italian and German forces, supported by 25 tanks, pushed back the defenders who lost around 600 men.

The following day, the 16th Infantry and 1st Armored units, in positions blocking the road to Tebessa, came up against the enemy spearhead and forced it to withdraw, taking 300 prisoners in the process. On the 22nd, the Germans had already withdrawn via Kasserine. At the beginning of March, the Fighting First was

Right. The Division marches towards Gafsa across a desert landscape.

Bottom. 18th Infantry fighting positions at El Guettar along the Gabès road. The crates next to the foxholes contain British combat rations.

relieved by the 9th Infantry Division and went to Morsott, west of Tebessa, to rest. With all of its units together for the first time, the Division was able to lick its wounds and receive a large intake of reinforcements.

El Guettar

The Division then attacked Gafsa on 17 March, captured the town and chased after the fleeing Italian garrison. The following day, it was sent in to attack the Gabès road towards the oasis of El Guettar. After a few clashes with the Italian 'Centauro' division, the 18th and 26th Infantry took up positions on the surrounding high ground. They were, however, subjected to day-long Luftwaffe raids and several artillery batteries were hit. On the morning of 23 March 1943, fire could be heard in the valley to the west of El Guettar. Actually, the 18th Infantry and the 601st Tank Destroyer Battalion had been hit full on by the 10. Panzer-Division. This epic fight, part of the Division's folklore, was later portrayed in the movie "Patton". The Germans, advancing from Kairouan, were determined to close the breach left open by the Italians. The forward lines were broken through and artillery positions threatened, but the GI's held on in their foxholes and the anti-tank guns (75mm guns mounted on half-tracks) succeeded in knocking out at least ten tanks. The enemy was slowed down by freshly-laid mines, placed by the 1st Engineers. By mid-morning, the Germans finally stalled. Also, American reinforce-

First Team infantrymen pass through Gafsa which was recaptured from the enemy on 18 March 1943.

COMPANY K/16th INFANTRY ON HILL 394

For several hours, the 16th was pinned down in front of a strongly held hill. In the same area, General MacNair, commanding Army Ground Forces in the USA and on an inspection round, was wounded by shell splinters on 23 April.

At hill 394, company K was stuck in a wheat field at its foot. Lieutenant Richard Cole, its commander, was hit in both legs while lying prone among his men. Medics could not venture out to fetch him, so he used his head. He made at tourniquet of his handkerchief, and using a fountain pen as a lever he twisted the tourniquet and held it, and at the same time began slowly crawling to the rear.

Sometime during the night, he felt a telephone wire that he cut. For twenty hours he waited until the signalmen found him at last.

When Lieutenant Antonelli found out that Cole was badly wounded, he took over the unit. At dusk, he went around the foot of the hill with a few men, fixed bayonet and attacked the enemy from behind. Antonelli was hit by grenade fragments in the chest but strong leadership remained thanks to First sergeant Arthur Godwin, who took the objective. A few hours later, a replacement officer was sent down from battalion but General Allen, who heard about Godwin's exploits, gave him an immediate battlefield promotion.

ments were arriving, including M-10 Tank Destroyers of the 899th TD Bn and the 17th Field Artillery Battalion. The ground that had been lost was recaptured and several very aggressive patrols fought off. By late afternoon, the enemy attempted a fresh advance with infantry and tanks but this time the axis of advance was under intense fire from machine-guns and artillery. The GI's did not withdraw, but they expected a more crushing victory as only 7% of the 1,800 prisoners taken were German. The Fighting First was then forced into a slow and costly advance north of the Gabès road against an adversary highly experienced in defensive combat, as he would soon prove in Sicily. The difficult terrain and bad maps contributed to the difficulty encountered in maneuvering.

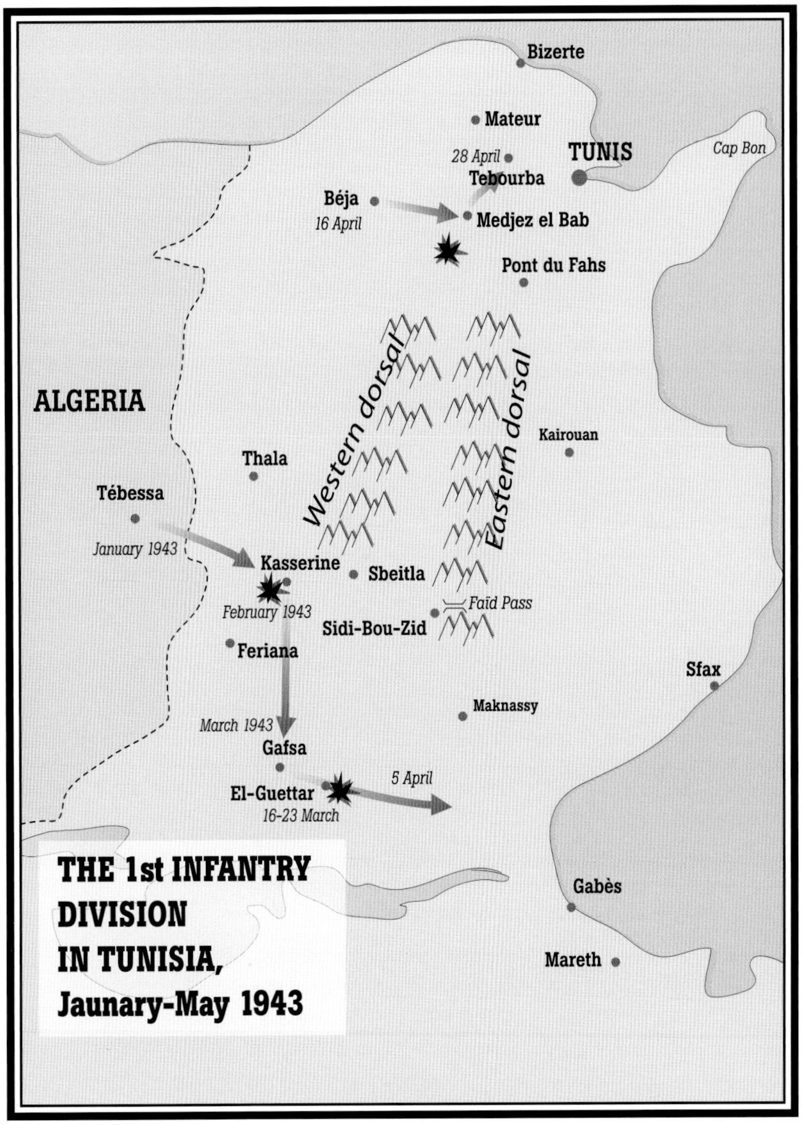

Top left.
General Terry Allen in conversation with French officers of the XIX corps on the Tunisian front at the beginning of 1943.

Left.
The photographer also took a picture of Brigadier General Theodore Roosevelt, Jr., the second in command of the 1st Division. Like his men, the general is scruffily-dressed against the wind and cold temperatures.

Victory in Tunisia

At dawn on 7 April 1943, the enemy broke off the fight. Making the most of this break, the Division went to Morsott for a rest period. It returned to the front-line at Beja on 16 April in terrain featuring low hills and wheat fields. The Tine valley, towards the north-west, would be its line of advance towards Bizerte. The German and Italian forces were now caught within a quarter-circle formed by Mateur, Bizerte, Tunis and Cap Bon. The British 1st and 8th Army were, in theory, tasked with the bulk of the fighting due to the wear and tear of the French and Americans. Nevertheless, on the night of 22 April, the 1st Division advanced towards the German 334. Infanterie-Division, the 'Barenthin' parachute engineers regiment and other ad-hoc infantry and armored units. Over the course of several days, the GI's, caught in a storm of shell fire, attacked the carefully fortified hills which changed hands several times. During the night of 24 April, the enemy with-

Right.
This heavily-armed halftrack has fallen victim to a Teller mine.

Below.
A GMC "Deuce and half" truck named 'Harry' has slipped off a road in Tunisia. Note the division tactical insignia on the door.

drew, mainly under the pressure of the 16th Infantry. In order to finish mopping up the right flank, the 2/18th Infantry and 1/13th Armored Infantry crossed the Tine river and took up positions on the surrounding hills. Cut-off on the opposite bank, the Americans were caught by a surprise counter-attack led by the Barenthin regiment. The fighting raged for five hours and it was impossible to send tanks across due to the steep banks. The Americans finally pulled back. After the war, Bradley blamed Allen for this costly attempt whereas it was he himself that had given the order to cross the river and attack nearby enemy forces. But on the morning of the 25th, it seemed obvious that the Germans had left the entrance to the valley. The 1st Division continued its advance, with the

34th Division on its left flank. As had been the case since the beginning of the campaign, the GI's had to seize an unending series of hills, which fell one after the other, but at the price of heavy casualties.

On 3 May, the 1st Armored Division took Mateur, which led to the collapse of German defenses in northern Tunisia. Up until 7 May, the Division maintained its advance along the river Tine on the enemy's northern flank, again facing the Luftwaffe paratroopers it was tasked with pinning down. Finally, the troops of Panzerarmee Afrika capitulated on 12 May and 130,000 German soldiers were captured. At the end of the campaign, the 1st Division was exhausted and most of the rifle companies were only at the strength of a large platoon. Over the last 17 days of fighting in Tunisia, it had lost 2,000 men!

Whilst the Allies were proudly parading in Tunis, the high command started receiving complaints concerning soldiers of the Fighting

Below.
30 June 1943, general Louis-Marie Koeltz, commander of the French XIX Corps, decorates generals Allen and Roosevelt with the Croix de Guerre for bravery during the Tunisian campaign. Allen remembered that he turned his head away when the French general came close to kiss him on the cheeks.

LT.-COLONEL CHARLES DENHOLM'S ODYSSEY

Lieutenant-colonel Charles J. Denholm, commanding the 1st Battalion/16th Infantry, had been captured during the fighting at Hill 523 near Mateur. He is seen here recovering after being rescued from the Italian ship that was taking him to Sicily with other Allied POWs. The boat was attacked by Allied planes and the crew jumped overboard outside of Tunis harbor.

Right. The divisional Provost Marshall, Major Lancer, in conversation with German soldiers at a POW enclosure in northern Tunisia, 8 May 1943.

First who were noisily and drunkenly celebrating. For its actions at Kasserine Pass, the 16th Infantry received a French army citation and its first American citation for the fighting at Mateur. The Division was transported in trucks to Oran to refit. At the end of May, it took part in exercises at the Amphibious Training Center in Port aux Poules, near Arzeu, and at Mers El Kebir. For the Big Red One had been pencilled in for Operation 'Husky,' the invasion of Sicily.

Patton clamors for the Big Red One

General George Patton, commander of the new 7th Army, had demanded that the 1st Infantry Division be part of his force. It was initially planned for the inexperienced 36th Infantry Division to land in the southern part of the island, but Patton complained about this to Eisenhower, saying *"I want those 1st Division sons-of-bitches, I won't go without them!"*. From 8-23 June, the Division made its way to Algiers and training continued with new amphibious maneuvers at Zeralda on the 23rd. The Division embarked on the ships and the convoys assembled off the coast of Tunis on 8 July.

Below.
At the end of the Tunisian campaign, the Division left for Oran where it refitted. This is where the men gained a reputation for bad discipline. The railroad car on the right bears the large number One of the Division in chalk.

Below.
The Division's anthem, 'The Big Red One,' was composed in Constantine in the summer of 1943 by Captain Donald T. Kellet as he was recovering from wounds received at El Guettar. Kellet served 30 years in the Army and was renowned for his military music.

4 - The invasion of Sicily

As part of the 7th US Army's II Corps, the 1st Division landed at Gela on 10 July 1943 and quickly overcame the Italian defenses.

However, the next day, it had to face a strong German-Italian counter-attack. The 'Livorno' division was tasked with breaking through to the sea from the north-west and the panzers of the 'Hermann Göring' division from the north-east. The tanks succeeded in advancing between the 2nd and 3rd Battalions of the 26th Infantry around seven o'clock in the morning. Phoning from the regimental HQ, General Roosevelt asked Terry Allen for immediate tank support. The landing of the Cannon companies from the three regiments was expedited, as well as several Sherman tanks of the 2nd Armored Division. In the 18th Infantry sector, the most had been made of nightfall to advance 25 kilometers. Battery B of the 33rd Field Artillery fired all of its shells at the tanks before being forced to withdraw. Taking up enfilade positions a little further back and having replenished its ammunition, it continued firing. Whilst this was taking place, the bridgehead was under constant Luftwaffe attack and several ships were hit, thus disrupting the flow of materiel.

At midnight, when the German pressure was at its strongest, unfazed General Allen typically ordered a counter-attack. By 11 July, the panzers were now cut off and despite the chaos that they had caused, were lacking infantry support in order to hold on to the terrain. When the German infantry at last reached the tanks, there were not enough of the latter remaining to operate efficiently. Also, the Germans got out of their trucks under full observation and the Americans brought down a hail of shell fire upon them, including from ships off the beachhead. The Navy guns also hit troop concentration areas far inland. Throughout these crucial hours, the Big Red One was also able to call upon the assistance of the paratroopers of the 82nd Airborne. Despite their scattered nighttime drop, the paratroopers immediately began to harass the enemy. Those who reached the 1st Division lines helped strengthen its positions against the tank attacks. The divisional objective, the airfield at Ponte Olivo, was captured on 12 July.

The Big Red One then pushed inland, capturing Mazzarino and Niscemi on 14 July and Barrafranca the 16th. It then came up against stiff German resistance and, for the first time, the 26th Infantry came under the terrifying fire of the Nebelwerfer rocket-launchers. As usual, after having blocked the initial American onslaught, the Germans counter-attacked and a Panzer IV company threatened the 3rd Battalion. Waiting in ambush, the 70th Light Tank Battalion, that had just been attached to the

Previous page, top.
The 1st Infantry Division landing near Gela, Sicily, 10 July 1943.

Previous page, bottom and this page, top right.
Gela, 20 July 1943, Major General Allen making his way to 7th Army HQ.

Right.
General Patton, who could no longer bear being stuck off the bridgehead on board the command ship 'Monrovia,' landed at Gela on 11 July. He is seen here in conversation with Brigadier General Theodore Roosevelt Jr. near the divisional HQ; he witnessed the attack of the Italian tanks.

Right.
The 16th Infantry approaching Enna in the center of the island, 19 July, 1943.

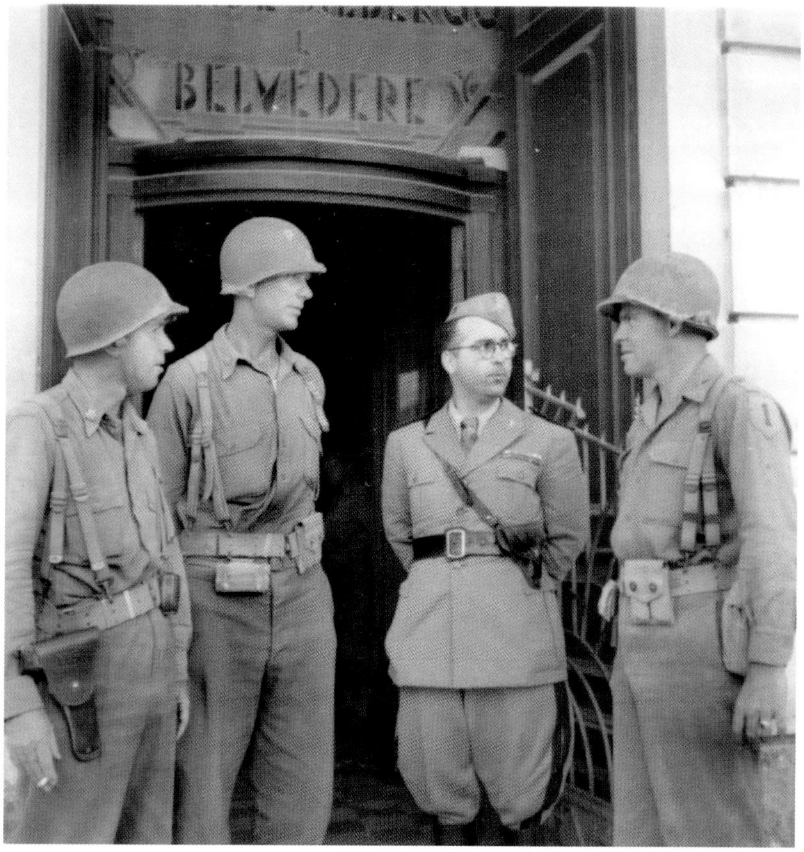

Below.
Enna, 21 July 1943, American officers and an Italian MSVN (Fascist Militia) officer coordinate law and order in the town. From left to right, Colonel R. Kilroe, Major Lancer of the Military Police and Captain R. Regan

Bottom, right.
Two 1st Division GI's give first aid to a wounded German soldier.

THE HERMANN GÖRING DIVISION'S LOST HONOR

A document captured later in the campaign illustrates its problems after it had been rebuilt after North Africa. In this field order, general Conrath, its commander, declares:

"I had the bitter experience to watch scenes which are not worthy of a German soldier, particularly not of a soldier of the Panzerdivision Hermann Göring.

Persons came running to the rear, hysterically crying, because they had heard the detonation of a single shot fired somewhere in the landscape. Others, believing in false rumours, moved whole columns to the rear. I want to state that these acts were committed not only by the youngest soldiers, but also by NCOs and warrant officers.

Panic, 'Panzer fear' and the spreading of rumours are to be eliminated by the severest measures. Withdrawal without orders, and cowardice, are to be punished on the spot, and, if necessary, by the use of weapons.

I shall apply the severest measures of court-martial against such saboteurs of the fight for freedom of our nation, and I shall not hesitate to give death sentences in serious cases."

Right. General Allen (left), looks at a map along with his superior officer, Omar Bradley, commander of the 2nd Army Corps. For some reason, whoever was standing between them has been covered over in ink by the censor.

1st, succeeded in destroying several tanks. With the divisional reconnaissance squadron, the light tank battalion then formed a mobile group which sped off to capture important crossroads in the Division's path. The next objective was Enna, the ancient capital of the island and the German forces' HQ. The 70th, accompanied by the 16th Infantry, entered the town on 20 July. The Division continued its advance towards the north, capturing an increasing number of Italian soldiers. As for the Germans, they withdrew under the cover of darkness after having systematically left behind a rear-guard in order to block the roads. Any obligatory points of passage were systematically booby-trapped with anti-tank Teller mines and 'Bouncing Betty' S-Mines. Whenever

GIs of the I/16 Infantry halt at Nicosia, 28 July 1943.

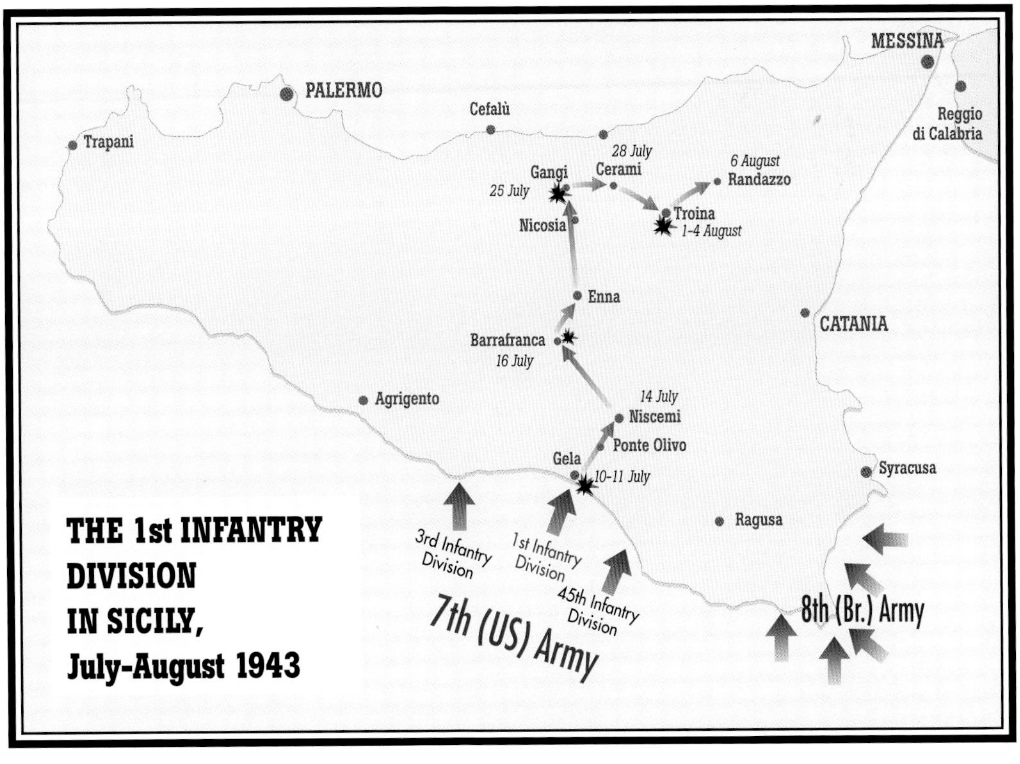

Right. Barrafranca, 19 July 1943,the Division's Provost Marshall, Major T. Lancer, dictates his orders to an NCO of the Military Police platoon.

Below. Major Lancer issues orders to his subordinates. Note the markings on his jeep's windshield.

Bottom right.
Private John H. Christopher, a motorcyclist with the divisional MP platoon. Note his armband with the unit's insignia.

possible, the GI's were transported by truck in order to keep chasing the enemy as closely as possible. By 24 July, the outskirts of Gangi had been reached.

However, it appeared that the Germans wanted to put up a fight there. On the same day, the Division was joined by 280 French Goumiers of the 4e GTM who were tasked with covering the north flank in the mountains where there were no usable tracks. In the area, the men of the 1st Engineers had the nasty surprise of coming across hundreds of the new wooden 'Holzmine 42' anti-tank mines, of which 35% were fitted with anti-lifting devices. Bitter fighting for Hill 937 took place and the Americans were forced back from it at dawn on 26 July. All around Gangi, the Americans attacked the high ground, particularly on the 28th when, with the aid of several light and medium tanks, they hit the defenders hard. The Fighting First regiments then reached Sperlinga, Cerami and Nicosia. In the latter town, 700 Italians of the 'Aosta' division were taken prisoner.

On 29 July, the 39th Infantry and the 26th Field Artillery of the 9th Division were attached to the 1st Division. This happened in the nick of time because the men under Terry Allen's command were about to experience their toughest fighting of the campaign.

The Battle of Troina

The 39th Infantry launched its attack on the strategic crossroads of Troina on 31 July 1943. They were, however, repulsed by the solidly entrenched German defenders. Bradley and General Allen then planned a large-scale maneuver.

The 26th Infantry, commanded by Colonel

(Continued on page 28)

Another Military Police motorcyclist, Private First Class Norman Ridge. The rider and the Harley Davidson are covered with the fine dust of the Sicilian roads.

Sergeants W. Kalette and V. Burns of the 16th Infantry hunt for snipers in the hill-top town of Troina, 6 August 1943.

Below. One of the Division's "mule skinners" feeding his companion. Contrary to the British, the Americans had learned the lessons of the Tunisian campaign, as even a jeep could not go everywhere. At Troina and other places, the mules enabled rations, water and ammunition to be brought up to front-line units.

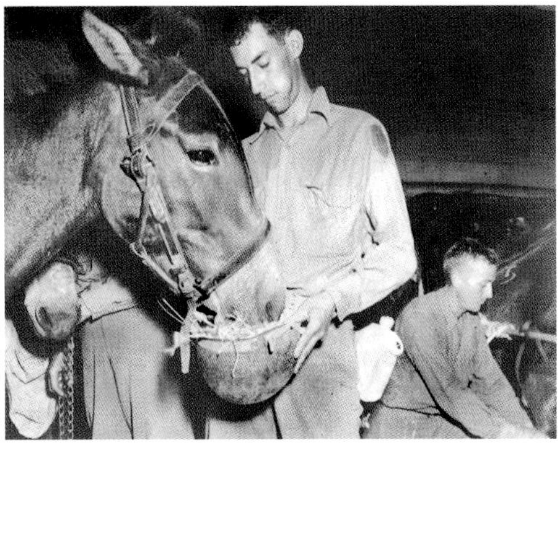

Top. Enna, 30 July 1943. Gaetano Niccosis (a former worker at the Pennsylvania shipyards), welcomes 1st Division soldiers with the star-spangled banner.

Above and opposite. During the advance towards Troina, the infantry moved in a series of rushes. The enemy positions were first hit by artillery, throwing up a pall of smoke and dust.

THE FIGHTING FOR TROINA

War correspondent Don Whitehead had reported the war for the Associated Press since the Desert battles in 1942. In this article, he writes about the battle for Troina.

"It was already dark when we reached the top of the ridge and found the battalion's advance command post preparing for the final drive to break the enemy's strong positions before Troina. One attack from the northwest had failed to shake the enemy loose from its hold on the strategic crossroads city, and now a pincer movement was under way to envelop him and smash his pockets of resistance on the ridges and in the valleys before us.

This battalion, under Maj. Charles (Chuck) Horner [1] was to drive straight to Troina. Another was swinging in from our right and a third from the left to cut roads leading out of the city to the east.

Below us in the wheat stubble, Pvt. Finley an Sgt. Fiarowitch are sweeping for mines.

"The Germans are booby-trapping their mines » Finley said, « But they are not using as many as they did in Tunisia."

The command post was in a culvert. Lieutenant Groves entered the post, grunting as he sat down. "What's the matter?" someone asked. "Hell, I went through all the shooting that morning and then sprained my back in a fall" Groves said. "The dirty bastards won't let me get our wounded off the field. If you go after the wounded they shoot at you. If a wounded man wiggles they shoot at him again."

Up the hill came a pack train of mules carrying ammunition, food and water. The Army requisitioned the long-eared transports from Sicilian farmers to carry supplies up ridges where jeeps are unable to travel. "These are smart mules" Groves said. "On that last ridge we were bringing up mortar ammunition when a mortar shell burst nearby. One of the mules fell down. We thought he was killed, but pretty soon we went back and found him grazing on the hillside. The mule naturally took cover whenever there was a shell blast near him."

Capt. Moorehouse came along the ridge road with his company, going into position for attack. Other companies were turning off the road below us and dark forms walked silently through night. We did not have to wait long to know the enemy still was on the ridge ahead. There was the crackle of machine gun fire. German flares illuminated the sky. Behind Troina a great fire blazed. Our artillery had connected with something, probably a fuel dump.

The battalion was unable to make any progress. We wrapped ourselves in blankets and lay down by the roadside to wait for dawn. Tracer bullets from machine gunners below us raked the enemy positions. Figures dashed out of hiding and ran over behind the ridge. "Get McCarthy up here" Horner said. "He's the best damned mortar man in this man's army. He'll get'em off there. With six mortars, that guy can get sixty shots in the air before the first shell lands. He can drop them in a rain barrel"

"There's a tank or halftrack shooting at our man over here!" someone said.

No sooner were the words spoken than a shell screamed into the hill twenty yards from us, and shrapnel buzzed over our heads. The enemy gunner had seen us on the road. We ran for cover and circled around the hill.

Glancing up as we passed a little stone shelter, I saw a soldier who seemed to be praying. He was kneeling with his hands outstretched. Then I saw a bullet had stopped his hands as they reached for a weapon. He was a German machine gunner."

1. The 16th Infantry's third Battalion. Horner won a DSC at Troina.

This page. Men of Company A of the 16th Infantry advance through Troina in order to capture stragglers and snipers, 6 August 1943.

Above. A Sicilian carabinier gives a drink to a parched 16th infantry soldier.

Right. A 16th Infantry medic comforts a German soldier wounded during the fighting for Troina.

John Bowen, was to outflank the town by taking Monte Basilio a few kilometers to the north. From there, the regiment would be in a position to cut off the retreat of enemy forces. The 26th advanced with artillery support, but the German guns fired back and the mountainous terrain slowed down any progression. On the morning of the following day, a battalion lost contact in the hilly terrain and wandered about for the rest of the day. A second battalion reached Monte Basilio with few losses, but then found itself under enemy bombardment from the neighboring hills. The 115. Panzergrenadier-Regiment launched a counter-attack to retake the high ground, but was forced back by machine-gun fire. The Germans were determined to hold on to Troina for as long as possible and, from 4 to 6 August, the troops positioned on Monte Basilio were pinned down. Attempts to resupply were only half successful. On 5 August, supplies and ammunition began to run low and the unit was weakened. It was at

Mistretta, 30 July 1943. Goumiers of the 4e GTM saddle-up their mules. These light and mobile mountain troops were tasked with guarding the flanks of the Division as it advanced. They also played a vital role in the fighting for Troina.

THE GENERAL WAS TOO CLOSE TO HIS MEN

On 7 August 1943 and at the time when his division had at last captured Troina, Terry Allen was relieved of this command.

As early as the Tunisian fighting, when Omar Bradley took command of the American IInd Corps, a serious clash of personalities opposed the two generals. One day or another, Bradley would bring him and his soldiers into line as Allen and his division were as one.

The 1st Division had experienced very tough fighting since the North African landings and had suffered from the decisions of a high command clumsily shared between the British and Americans.

Thus, the Division had forged itself a well-affirmed personality in adversity. The GIs of the Big Red One felt that they were relentlessly given the bulk of the hard work. Allen and his second in command, T. Roosevelt, were very close to their men, something which no doubt strengthened the esprit de corps, but one which also encouraged a sense of superiority that did not sit well with the team spirit that had to permeate throughout the entire army. A GI of the said 16th Infantry : "The men knew that they were good. We were all full of fight because we were sure that our division was Number One in everything. Each soldier helped his comrades. We all knew each other and shared our personal problems. We had become like a family."

Allen had confided in one of his officers that : "My guys know that are capable of whooping the Hun's asses whenever they want. Take any one of them, from truck drivers, infantrymen, artillerymen, they are all excellent fighters."

Like many Americans of their generation, Allen and his deputy Roosevelt, liked a drink and neither of them had the presence and smartness of a George Patton, for example. Bradley described Allen during a visit to the divisional staff mess in Tunisia : "Terry was sat at the table, his black hair was uncombed and his face had a thin smile. He was wearing s strange greenish uniform; his batman had stitched the pleats on his pants, which in any case was totally creased. The general's stars on his shirt had been taken from an Italian POW's collar tabs."

By force of habit and in solidarity with his men, Allen slept in a tent and sometimes even on the ground. The war correspondent, Ernie Pyle, himself close to the men, could see the effort that Allen was making to reduce the divide between officers and men : "As far as I know, Terry Allen was the only general to sleep on the ground. All the others had camp beds or managed to sleep in houses. He made all of his headquarters staff do the same as even the fold-up camp beds took up too much space in the trucks and this space could be put to better use (...). In his tent there was a sleeping bag on the ground that took up half the space. The other half was taken up by a canteen of water held up with stones over a fuel stove, and by a fold-up table."

Already tired at the end of the Tunisian campaign, it is beyond dispute that Terry Allen was ill-tempered and borderline insubordinate towards Bradley. He privately referred to Bradley as being a "bible basher". Therefore, at the end of the Sicilian campaign, Bradley requested to Eisenhower to relieve Allen and Roosevelt of their commands. Patton had already suggested this a short time before but, due to his respect for Allen, had not insisted. Bradley officially justified his request by the difficulties encountered by the 1stDivision in its capture of Troina.

The tired commander of the Big Red One deserved to be replaced, but this created a scandal due to the way in which Bradley settled his scores – as well as with Patton – in his memoirs that were published at the end of his life. He stigmatized Allen's alcoholism and his rebellious ways, as well as his men's lack of discipline. It is true that GIs of the Fighting First, when at rest in Oran before Sicily, had beaten up rear-echelon personnel and had demolished bars in memorable brawls. They were in a very bad mood when the rumor was going around that they were to return home after Africa. Also, Bradley did not issue the order face to face, but rather via a letter that arrived with other routine orders to the divisional HQ. Informed by his chief of staff, Allen took it badly but nevertheless returned to his post to finish off his work. Somewhat embarrassed, Bradley informed him by telephone that he would remain with his men until the capture of Troina. Upon Patton's insistence, Allen's transfer was not to be made under the guise of a disciplinary sanction and it was planned that he would take command of another division in the United States.

In a letter to his wife, the general, even though he was delighted to return home and see his wife, wrote that : "It hurts to leave the Fighting First. We have been through difficult times together and the whole team has shown faultless loyalty on good and bad days. Our guys have marched and fought constantly for 27 days and at least 14 nights 1.Their endurance in the face of such terrible difficulties almost brings me to tears."

At first called back to Oran, Allen was decorated with the Distinguished Service Medal, a puny reward for what his division had accomplished. In a message to his men, he said : "I am happy to have had the honor to command you. You should be proud of your exploits as you have been true to your motto : 'Nothing in hell can stop the 1st Division !'".

---

1. Despite being a cavalry officer at the outset, Allen had spent a long time studying infantry combat and had elaborated intricate tactics for night fighting. He applied these with success in Sicily, then in Germany with the 104th Division.

Left. At the divisional command post near Cerami, 4 August 1943. General Allen explains the situation at Troina to war correspondents Clark Lea (center) and Don Whitehead (right).

Right. At the divisional command post at Cerami, Terry Allen in conversation with Lt.Col. Flint of the 39th Infantry. This 9th Division regiment was tasked with the first assault on Troina but, despite its fighting ability, was unable to push the Germans out. Colonel "Paddy" Flint was later killed in Normandy on the front-line, on 23 July 1944.

Above. In this photo, taken at the same location on 4 August, Troina can be seen in the distance under shell fire.

Below. General Allen with some of his staff. On the left is General Clift Andrus, the divisional artillery commander.

Above. A view of Troina from the north-west, with mount Etna to the left in the background. The town can be seen on the crest in the center of the horizon line.

this moment that the German infantry launched a fresh attack and the area became the scene of bitter fighting. Private James W. Reese set up his mortar squad and began firing furiously at the attackers. With his last three projectiles, Reese knocked out a machine-gun, then continued to engage the enemy with his Garand rifle, before being mortally wounded by shell splinters. For his heroism, Pte. Reese of the 26th Infantry, was posthumously awarded the Medal of Honor. Given the crushing pressure of the American troops and their incapacity to push back the 26th Infantry from its positions threatening their withdrawal route, the enemy pulled out of Troina during the night of 6 August and withdrew towards Randazzo. The 9th Infantry Division began the pursuit, whilst the 1st Division moved away for a well-deserved rest period. Some of its units had lost more than half of their strength at Troina. However, this victory opened the way to the Messina Strait. On 7 August, the 1st Division was placed

Above. A 1st Division soldier takes a look at a German rocket in its launcher, usually fitted to the side of a half-track. Initially designed to lay down smoke on the battlefield, there were also explosive versions of this rocket which flew through the air with a terrifying shriek.

Left.
In a street in Troina that has escaped destruction, men of I/16th Infantry eat at the company kitchen.

Right. Randazzo, 13 August 1943, the moment when the British and Americans linked up behind Etna. From left to right : Colonel George A. Smith (18th Infantry Regiment), Colonel 'Paddy' Flint of the 39th Infantry (attached to the 1st for the capture of Troina), Major General Vyvyan Evelegh (British 78th Division) and Brigadier General E. E. Cass (8th Infantry Brigade).

in II Corps reserve. However, the men were in for a shock that day as they lost their commander. Indeed, the hugely popular Terry Allen was relieved by Bradley and replaced by Major-General Clarence R. Huebner. After 37 days of relentless combat, the Division had taken part in the capture of 18 towns and had taken 5,935 prisoners. Its total casualties were 264 killed, 1,184 wounded and 337 missing.

On the following 23 October, the 1st Division received movement orders that would take it to England in order to prepare for Operation 'Overlord,' the invasion of Normandy. Thus, throughout the winter and the following spring, the GI's would take part in further amphibious exercises and maneuvers in the English countryside.

"VARSITY-OLD RELIABLES"

Right.
General Patton addresses men of the Big Red One at Licata after the conquest of Sicily. He had been forced by Eisenhower to apologize to each division for his behavior whilst visiting two field hospitals. Indeed, he had hit shell-shocked soldiers, calling them cowards. The men of the 1st Division listened to his speech in polite silence as they considered the incident closed. However, at the 9th Division, Patton barely started speaking before the GI's began excitedly shouting "Georgie! Georgie!" in admiration. Patton left the platform with tears in his eyes and returned to his car in view of the entire parade, standing stiffly to attention...

?

Left.
General Theodore Roosevelt jr. and his jeep 'Rough Rider' seen here in Prata, Italy, January 1944. Transferred by Bradley, he was, for a short time, attached as liaison officer with the Canadians. 'Rough Rider' is in reference to the cavalry troops led by his father during the war against Spain in Cuba in 1898.

5 - Omaha Beach and the liberation of France

"The United States Army is made up of the 1st Division and four million replacements."

Said an American general, complaining about the division to T. Roosevelt Jr., who impishly replied, "But isn't that the case?"

As part of the Normandy invasion, the Big Red One was tasked with landing on Omaha Beach with the 29th Infantry Division.

Above.
From left to right, Colonel George A. Taylor (commanding the 16th Infantry), Major Carl W. Plitt, Major Charles E. Tegtmeyer (the 16th Infantry surgeon, who won the DSC on Omaha Beach), Major John H. Lauten and Captain William Friedman, during maneuvers in England, a few weeks prior to D-Day.

Left.
24 February 1944, men of the 16th Infantry undergoing amphibious training at the Assault Training Center in Devon where all the invasion combat units underwent at least one course.

Below.
Men of the Regiment descend down nets, placed along the flanks of troopship's hull, and into landing craft during an exercise.

Opposite.
16th Infantry soldiers landing on Slapton Sands, 4 May as part of Operation Fabius, a dress rehearsal of the invasion.

But first let us go back several months in time in Sicily. On 21 October 1943, the Division embarked on several ships and, two days later, their destination was announced, England. A lot of the GI's thought that they would be invading Italy and some even hoped that they were to set sail for home. It had been just over a year since the boys of the Big Red One had left England for North Africa when they returned close to Liverpool where they were met on the quayside by a British band.

One example is that of Company E, 16th Infantry who set up in a tented camp for the winter at Walditch, a few kilometers from the Channel. When off-duty, the soldiers went for strolls and watched movies. It was often rainy and British and American military police patrolled the town day and night. The local population was very welcoming to Uncle Sam's soldiers and some romance even blossomed. For Christmas Eve, turkey was served in the battalion mess hall, along with ice cream and plenty of beer. Religious men went to church at Bridport for the sunday service. The weather was cold and the GI's began their street combat training in a vicinity that had been destroyed by air raids near the port of Weymouth. In January 1944, General Montgomery inspected the Regiment at the Bridport cricket ground and stated that: *"Of all the American divisions that I have seen, I'd rather go to war with the 1st Division"*.

In February 1944, the infantrymen began their amphibious training courses at Woolacombe (Devon), learning how to attack fortified positions, obstacle destruction and so on. The entire 16th Infantry took part in a large-scale exercise on the 24th. This type of training continued up to March with infantry deployment and tactical exercises in the surrounding countryside. On 2 April, General Eisenhower gave a speech that dispelled any illusions about returning to the United States. He said that the *"1st Division would be one of the last divisions to return home, I'm going to keep you as a good luck charm"*. From this moment onwards, the First Team was placed on full alert for the invasion of Europe. The troops of the 1th Bn landed on Slapton Sands on 4 May as part of exercise Fabius I, a large-scale rehearsal for the landings on the Normandy coast.

The companies were organized into five assault boat teams, structured in such a way as to take place in a small landing craft and armed with flame-throwers, Bangalore torpedoes and demolition charges. Embarkation began on 1 June in the ports of southern England.

Below, officers of the 26th Regimental Combat Team for 6 June, from left to right: Lieutenant-Colonel F.J. Murdoch (1st Battalion/26th), Lieutenant-Colonel Derrill M. Daniel (2nd Battalion), Colonel J. Seitz (commanding officer), Lieutenant-Colonel J. Corley (3rd Battalion) and Lieutenant-Colonel Bryde (commander of the 33rd Field Artillery Battalion).

Above. Staff Sergeant Philip Streczyk (right) and his men, enjoy a rest outside an English pub during training somewhere in Southern England. Streczyk would receive the Distinguished Service Cross for his actions on Omaha Beach.

Omaha Beach

Omaha Beach was one of two American sectors. 5.9 kilometers in length, it included the localities of Vierville-sur-Mer in the west, and Saint-Laurent-sur-Mer in the center, with the villages of Colleville-sur-Mer and Grand Hameau to the east. A plateau overlooked the beach and there were four draws that formed natural passageways inland. The 16th Infantry, and the 116th Infantry of the 29th Division, were designated to land on the beach that was divided into four sectors from west to east: Charlie, Dog, Easy and Fox. After the simultaneous raids on the batteries at Pointe du Hoc,

Below.
The 32nd Field Artillery Battalion halted along an English road awaiting the order to move towards the seaside ports. The 105mm M3 howitzers have been named with 1st Division battle honours: Djebel Berda-Mt Etna and Hill 407 for the gun in the middle of the photo.

Above. This howitzer has been named 'Oran' and 'Troina'. The gun has been prepped for an amphibious assault with the breech and main mechanical elements sealed with an asbestos paste that will have to be entirely removed before firing.

3 June 1944, Captain Larry Deery, the 16th Infantry chaplain, holds a service on the deck of the command ship, USS Ancon.

these regiments would be able to be reinforced by the 2nd and 5th Rangers battalions. The operation was placed under General Leonard T. Gerow, the commander of V Corps, 1st Army (General Bradley).

As day broke on June 6, thick smoke caused by the Navy bombardment hid the French coast, and shell fire from the ships against the Atlantic Wall was as inaccurate as the bombers' strikes. From their vantage point on the troopships, the soldiers believed however that the Germans would be crushed beneath tons of earth. But this was not the case and the enemy fortifications were still very much intact. At 06.30 hrs, the 16th Infantry landed in front of Colleville-sur-Mer. The Germans, safe inside their concrete bunkers, poured fire into the attacking troops and the operation was a hair's breadth away from catastrophe. Losses were huge for the first assault wave; 95% of the officers were dead. In the chaos, units became mixed up and were pinned down on the beach.

Below. A 2,5 ton truck belonging to an unidentified 1st Division unit bears a yellow and black tactical marking on its door, painted in the middle of the star.

Following page, top. Another photograph showing embarkation in the same Landing Ship Tank (LST).

Above.
Private Clyde Peacock of the 1st Military Police Platoon, is seen here on embarkation in June 1944. Note the flag on the jeep's windshield which also bears the instructions for removing the wading equipment and waterproofing paste.

Left.
Reversing into the hold of an LST, this ambulance bears the yellow and black markings of the 1st Medical Battalion on its fender and door.

Above. The 1/16th, probably Company C, lands at Easy Red at high tide around 07.30 hrs. The shoreline appears to be choked up. One can make out demolition teams dealing with the obstacles, and also a Sherman tank in the center.

Below.
Men of the 1st Battalion, 16th Infantry, in a Coast Guards LCVP heading for Omaha Beach. The boat team leader, behind the bow ramp, looks over to the coast.

Opposite page, top.
6 June 1944, LCVP craft carrying the 1st Division off the coast of Normandy in the Easy Red sector.

On Easy Red, the 16th Infantry had been almost bled white and the survivors sheltered behind a shingle bank. The shoreline was covered with equipment, the dead and the dying and there was no space in which to send reinforcements. However, the veterans of North Africa and Sicily refused to accept defeat. General Taylor, commanding the regiment, stood up and bellowed something that has entered into legend: "*Two kinds of people are staying on this beach: those who are dead and those who are going to die. Now let's get the hell out of here!*"

Slowly, the men left the shoreline and began moving inland. At around 11am, there were more and more penetrations and hundreds of soldiers began to attack the positions overlooking the beach. The 18th Infantry, having just landed at the Easy sector, gained the high ground and began to advance towards Colleville-sur-Mer, where it joined the 16th Infantry already fighting there. A bunker enfilading the beach became the 'Danger Forward' command post ('Danger' was the codeword designating the 1st Division). The 16th Infantry had suffered a 30% casualty rate in the first hour of fighting but by the evening of 7 June, the Overlord objectives had been partially reached. The enemy had been pushed back, except in the Formigny-Trévières sector.

On 8 June, the 26th Infantry continued its advance on the left flank, towards Tour en Bessin. Its 3rd Battalion took to the Bayeux road towards Sainte-Anne, where it stayed for the night. A German column, heading from the north, accidentally entered into the American positions around three in the morning, leading

to hand-to-hand combat. The situation was finally stabilized thanks to field and naval artillery. Company L suffered heavy losses when two German trucks, filled with prisoners from this unit, were destroyed by naval shells. On 9 June, intelligence reports indicated the possibility of a strong enemy concentration, including tanks, in Cerisy forest. The Saint-Lô-Bayeux road was reached on the 10th. Enough ground had been captured to guarantee the safety of the beachheads.

(Continued on page 42)

Below. These GI's of the 1st Infantry Division are waiting in landing craft in Weymouth before transferring to transport ships heading for France.

CLARENCE HUEBNER, A NEW COACH FOR THE BIG RED ONE

At the end of the Sicily campaign, Terry Allen was replaced by General Huebner who was tasked by Bradley with restoring order to the division. Clarence Huebner was an officer who had risen through the ranks from private to general and who had occupied almost all command positions, from the rifle squad, to the infantry regiment (read his biography page 89).

Huebner was posted to Algiers in 1943 on the staff of British general Harold Alexander (15th Army Group), serving as the American counterpart of his chief of staff. During the hasty preparation of the Sicily landings, Huebner found it difficult to work with the indecisive personality of his superior and was found to be lacking in the diplomacy required for the position. Added to this, Alexander at this time, had a poor opinion of American soldiers and ended up sacking his judgemental subordinate fifteen days before the landings. Briefly unassigned, Huebner was soon chosen by Bradley as a replacement for Terry Allen.

Huebner was a forthright officer, with a leadership style based on organization, planning and attention to detail. Bradley counted on him to get the Division back on track, especially concerning discipline. No sooner had he taken command did he put into place a regime of exercise and drill. He insisted in particular on the regulation salute. Every evening in the mess, the new commander tore a strip off any officers that he deemed unsatisfactory. His outlook was straightforward: *"It should not be forgotten that the American soldier is fundamentally a civilian in uniform. He is stubborn and individualistic and whatever the impression he gives, he is sure that he is smarter than the others. Even if we tell him the contrary, he will always do as he pleases."*

Having himself risen through the ranks from a private, Huebner knew full well the limits and feelings of the men under his command. Thus, he could define the limits of empathy and decide when he could push the men a little harder or whether it required holding back.

Before leaving for England, Chief of Staff, Colonel Stanhope B. Mason, stated that: *"The changes were over. The Division was now a close-knit team. No-one had been fired, no-one had been shot. The time when meals were eaten in icy silence was over..."*

Nicknamed "Coach", Huebner continued training the Division his own way and helped it retain its elite status, from Normandy and on to Germany.

Sicily, July 1943. General Huebner, the new commander of the 1st Division, seen here with the 7th Army commander, George Patton.

Opposite and following page. These 1st Division GI's, on board a Coast Guards transport ship, give their equipment a final check. The Division's shoulder patch can be seen on the shoulder of the GI in the foreground to the right. Note the waterproof bags for the gas mask worn on the chest and the vinyl bags in which they place their rifles. We do not know the unit to which these men, armed with the old Springfield 1903 rifle, belonged.

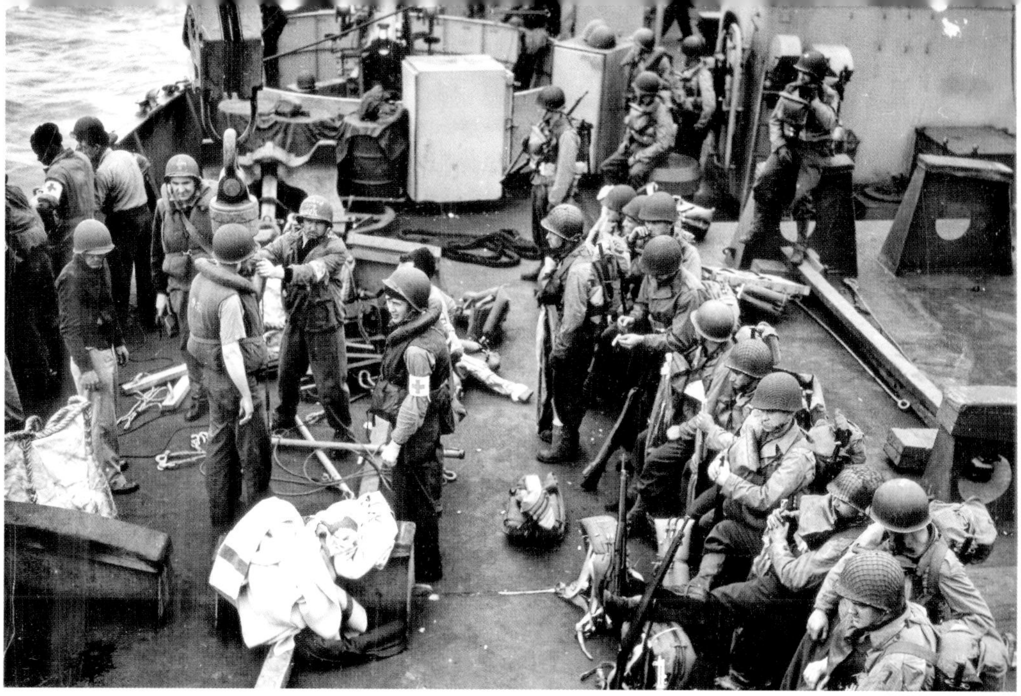

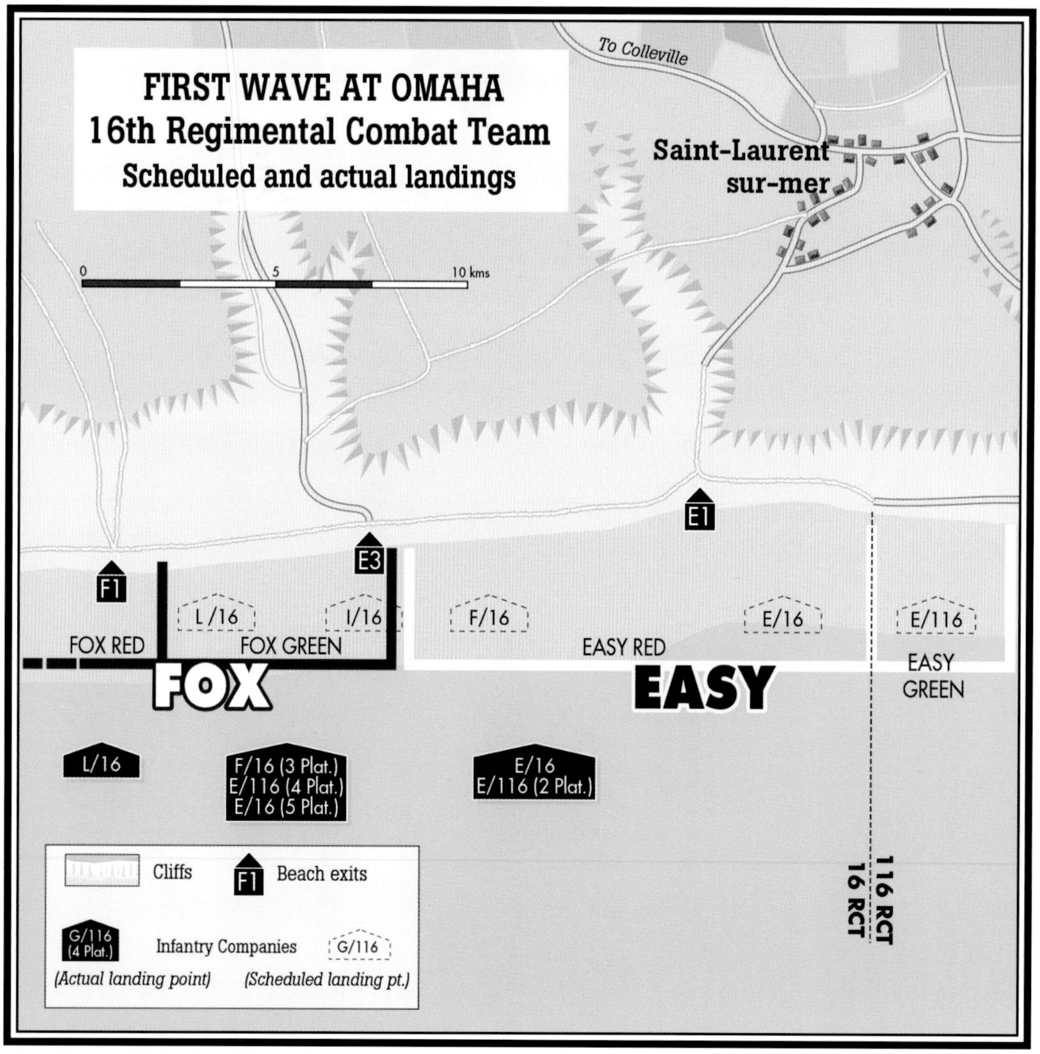

Map taken from "Spearheading D-Day – American special units in Normandy" by Jonathan Gawne, Histoire & Collections 2011.

The 18th Infantry preparing to land on Omaha Beach at the Easy Red sector.

Above. 6 June, beneath the WN-60 strong-point at the foot of the Colleville-sur-Mer cliffs, a machine-gun team from Company M, 16th Infantry, starts to move off the beach.

Top, right. A view of the Easy Red sector, taken in the afternoon of 6 June.

Caumont

The next phase of the advance required the capture of Caumont, 30 kilometers south of Omaha. This town and its vital road junction stood on some high ground in front of the Cerisy forest. Its capture would cut the German lines of communication between Caen, Saint-Lô, Vire and Avranches. The 18th and 26th Infantry attacked frontally with the 16th hanging back to lend support or protect the flanks. Supported by the Tank Destroyers of the 635th TD Bn and the Shermans of the 745 Tank Bn., the two spearhead regiments encountered, on the 12th, only a few mobile covering units comprising of

Beached off Colleville sur Mer, LCT-603 transported two Jeeps of the 32nd FA Bn, four of the 18th Infantry, and 17 jeeps with trailers of the 81st Chemical Mortar Battalion.

DON WHITEHEAD, A WAR CORRESPONDENT ON OMAHA BEACH

We meet Whitehead again after Sicily, this time on the morning of June 6, 1944. He landed on Omaha beach in General Wyman's (the division's assistant commander) boat.

"Soon we could see the beach – Easy Red beach – a hellish inferno of battle. Shells exploded in the surf and sent up small geysers while bullets whipped up ugly little spouts of water. The thunder of our naval gunfire and the explosion of shells rolled over us now (...) The situation ashore was bad, Everything was confused and behind schedule. Casualties were heavy. The engineers had not been able to clear all the gaps planned though the beach defenses. The invasion was stalled and somebody had to get in and help bring order out of the confusion.

Our coxswain found a gap through the barriers of barbed wire, logs, steel spokes and mines. Somehow we raced through the gap on the crest of a wave. The LCVP grounded and we ran down the ramp and waded through the surf to throw ourselves on the beach as thousands of others hugging that precious little strip of sand and gravel.

From the water's edge the beach shelved upwards for about 30 feet. Beyond this was a flat, open stretch rising gradually to a bluff less than 300 yards away. The beach was a shooting gallery and the men who came out of the sea were the targets.

Many officers were killed before they could reach shore. Units were scrambled and left without leaders and without direction. And so the men dug in on that narrow strip of beach washed by waves and blood. They piled up by the thousands, shoulder to shoulder (...) Nothing was moving on the beach.

I lay on the beach wanting to burrow into the gravel. And I thought: "*This time we have failed! God we have failed! Nothing has moved from this beach and soon, over that bluff, will come the Germans. They'll swarm down on us...*"

"*We've got to get these men off the beach*," Wyman said. "*This is murder!*"

Wyman studied the situation for a few minutes – and then, with absolute disregard for his own life and safety, he stood up to expose himself to the enemy's fire. Calmly, he began moving lost units in their proper positions, organizing leadership for leaderless troops. He began to bring order out of confusion and to give direction to this vast collection of inert manpower waiting only to be told what to do, where to go."

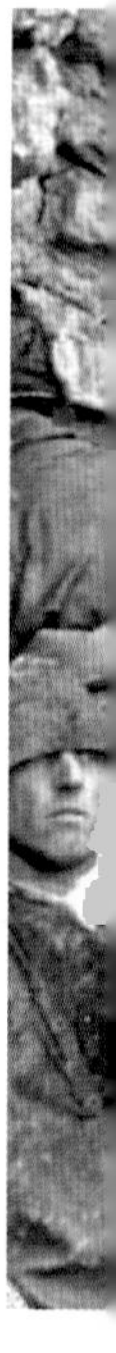

A haggard medic in the Fox Red sector finds shelter at the foot of the cliff on a narrow strip of shingle.

LCI-83, carrying elements of the 20th Engineers, off the F-1 exit (Cabourg draw) at approximately 08.30 hrs. To the left, we can see the fording kits of the two M4 tanks of the 741st Tank Battalion, probably those used by Lieutenant Monteith (L/16th Infantry) to give support to his men.

Below.
6 June, morning. 3rd Battalion, 16th Infantry men and wounded, mixed up with some 29th Division GI's, huddle together at the foot of the cliffs on the far-eastern edge of Omaha Beach. In a short while, the rising tide will reach the cliffs.

Above.
Another photograph of 1st and 29th Division men sheltering at the foot of the cliffs. On the right, a medic administers first aid to a wounded man.

Below.
One of the casemates built by the Germans to cover the beach with enfilade fire and protected from naval guns.

Below, right.
After the landings, the 16th Infantry set up its aid station in a German bunker in the Fox Green sector.

half-tracks and occasionally a tank. The Americans entered Caumont at dusk, but were repulsed. The next day, the Germans even had the nerve to push forward strong patrols to probe the American lines. At 15.00 hrs, the 33rd Field Artillery was called on to break up a new attack and it fired almost nine hundred 105mm shells on this day, compared to 39 the previous day. Up to that time, the identified enemy units in the sector were the remains of the 352. Infanterie-Division, 726. Grenadier-Regiment and the 30th mobile brigade. However, from 10 June onwards, elements of the 17th SS division "Götz von Berlichingen" appeared and on the 12th, the 3rd parachute (Fallschirmjäger) division arrived from Brest. By 14 June, the 5. Fallschirmjäger Regiment, 304. Panzergrenadier Regiment and the 38. Panzer-Pionier-Abt. (2. Panzerdivision), formed a semi-circle around Caumont. These were fresh troops with high morale. The next day, the Fallschirmjäger and engineers launched an attack against the positions

Omaha Beach seen from one the second wave landing craft. The coast is hidden by the scrub fires.

Right.
In the days following the landings at Omaha, soldiers of the 1st Division and the Engineer Special Brigade began removing the dead.

Below. Photo taken from a landing craft as it approaches the shore. The tide is high and barely covers the wrecks in front of the shoreline.

Bottom, right. In this photo, taken from a large Landing Craft Infantry at midday, we can see the Easy sector in front of Saint-Laurent sur-Mer, still hidden by the scrub fires caused by the naval shelling. It was at this time that the Division's second wave comprising of the 18th Infantry arrived. On the right, we can see LCI(L)553 that has run aground after hitting a mine and taking several 88 hits.

held by the 18th Infantry, with the latter repulsing the attack and inflicting heavy casualties. On 17 June, the Germans were expecting an enemy thrust in the sector and pulled back, however, as nothing happened, they returned once more towards the town. Up until 30 June, with the weather preventing the deployment of tactical aircraft, the enemy consolidated its positions. For the first time, both sides used psychological warfare with the use of leaflets placed inside shells. The German leaflets, illustrated with pornographic images, made the GI's laugh by their naivety. On 13 July, the division was relieved by the 5th Infantry Division and stayed at Colombières where the men prepared for a large-scale offensive.

Marigny

The American high command launched Operation Cobra on 25 July 1944. The aim was to break through the German front in the south of the Cotentin. At 9:40am, a huge aerial bombardment dropped over 3,300 tonnes of bombs as a prelude to the offensive. The ground forces launched their attack at 11am. However, after initial progress, the advance was held up by an unforeseen resistance and the Americans halted temporarily at nightfall. The following day, Airforce P-47 Thunderbolts hit numerous targets around Marigny. The tanks of the 3rd Armored Division resumed the offensive in the morning against elements of the "Götz von Berlichingen", "Panzer Lehr" and the 353. Infanterie-Division. In the course of the afternoon, tanks of the 2. SS Panzer-Division "Das Reich" , reinforced by elements of the 353. ID, launched a violent counter-attack around Marigny. Colonel George Smith Jr's 18th Infantry, supported by tanks, held off the repeated attacks and engaged in fierce fighting in the ruins of the small town.

But the Americans had a strong hold on the area by the end of the afternoon. The roads, blocked with numerous wrecked German vehicles, were cleared by bulldozers. After having liberated Marigny on the 27th and Camprond the following day, the Big Red One reached Brécey on 31 July and took control of the crossings over the river See. The 1st Army operational orders for 1 August 1944 stipulated that units were to continue the advance towards the south-east, except for V Corps which was to

Above. Photo taken shortly after 6 June in a 1st Division Message Center. Visible on the field table is the regulation clock that allowed for the taking down of the precise time messages were sent and received.

Left. 21 June, 1st Division engineers receive letters for the first time since D-Day.

Left.
A GMC CCKW 353 of the 33rd Field Artillery Battalion passes through Le Molay-Littry on the Balleroy road, 4 July 1944.

Above.
Generals Eisenhower and Bradley decorate men of the 16th Infantry with the Distinguished Service Cross at the divisional HQ near Balleroy, 2 July 1944. Major Tegtmeyer, the 16th Infantry medical officer, receives his medal from the Supreme Commander himself. On this day, 'Ike' stated to the GI's of the Big Red One: "I've been watching your exploits since North Africa and Sicily. I'm beginning to think that the 1st Division is my Praetorian guard."

Left.
General Bernard Montgomery, seen here on 7 July 1944, decorates Technical Sergeant Philip Streczyk (E/16) with the British Military Medal for his bravery on D-Day. He had been awarded with the American DSC at Balleroy on 2 July.

ORDER OF BATTLE OF THE 1st INFANTRY DIVISION IN NORMANDY

● Commanding General:
Major General Clarence R. Huebner
● Assistant CG: Brigadier
General Willard G. Wyman
● Chief of staff: Colonel Stanhope B. Mason
G-1: Lt Colonel Charles S. Ware
G-2: Lt Colonel Robert F. Evans
G-3: Lt Colonel Frederick W. Gibb
G-4: Lt Colonel Clarence M. Eymer
G 5: Lt Colonel John M. Rogers, Jr.
Adjudant General: Lt.-Colonel
Leonidas Gavalas

● 16th Infantry Regiment,
first wave unit on June 6
Colonel George A. Taylor
Executive officer:
Lt.-Colonel John Matthews
S-1 (Personnel): Capt. William Friedman
S-2 (Intelligence): Maj. John Lauten
S-3 (Operations): Maj. Carl Plitt
S-4 (Supply): Maj. Leonard Godfray
Surgeon: Maj. Charles Tegtmeyer

● 1st Battalion (transport: *USS Samuel Chase*, US Coast Guard)
Lt. Colonel Edmund Driscoll
Company A: Capt. James Pence
Company B: Capt. Thomas Merendino
Company C: Capt. Victor Briggs
Company D: Capt. Polydore Dion

● 2nd Battalion (transport: *USS Henrico*)
Lt. Colonel Herbert Hicks
Company E: Capt. Ed Wozenski
Company F: Capt. John Finke
Company G: Capt. Joseph Dawson
Company H: Capt. Robert Irvine

● 3rd Battalion (British transport: *SS Empire Anvil*)
Lt. Colonel Charles Horner
Company I: Capt. Kimball Richmond
Company K: Capt. Anthony Prucnal
Company L: Capt. John Armellino
Company M: Capt. Emil Edmonds

● 18th Infantry Regiment
Colonel George Smith, Jr.
1st Battalion: Lt. Colonel
Henry G. Leonard, Jr.
2nd Battalion: Lt. Colonel John Williamson
3rd Battalion: Lt. Colonel Courtney P. Brown

● 26th Infantry Regiment
Colonel John F. R. Seitz
1st Battalion: Lt. Colonel
Francis J. Murdock, Jr
2nd Battalion: Lt. Colonel Derrill M. Daniel
3rd Battalion: Lt. Colonel John T. Corley

● 1st Reconnaissance platoon,
mechanized: captain William L. Blake

● 1st Engineer Combat Battalion:
Lt. Colonel William B. Gara

● Divisional artillery:
Brigadier General Clift Andrus
5th Field Artillery Bn:
Lt. Colonel Robert N. Tyson
7th Field Artillery Bn:
Lt. Colonel George W. Gibbs
32nd Field Artillery Bn:
Lt. Colonel Edward S. Bechtold
33rd Field Artillery Bn:
Lt. Colonel Walter J. Bryde

● 1st Signal Company
● 701st Light Maintenance Ordnance
Co.: captain Raymond C. Huntoon
● 1st Quartermaster Company:
captain John J. King
● 1st Military Police Platoon:
Major Thomas F. Lancer
● 1st Medical Battalion:
Lt. Colonel Samuel Blechfeld

head towards Vire. The next day, VII Corps, to which the 1st Infantry Division belonged, had compressed the Brécey Pocket by around 8 km. On 4 August, it changed direction in order to threaten the enemy's rear and isolate its forces from Paris. Upon approaching Mortain, an important road junction on the Vire – Avranches road, the Fighting First came under intense crossfire from mortars and artillery. The town had to be held in order to prevent the enemy from breaking through to Avranches and the sea at the base of the Cotentin Peninsula. With the help of the 39th Infantry (9th Division), the

Below. Pte. Victor Dowdle (from Blackfoot, Idaho), a soldier with the 18th Infantry anti-tank company, paints his unit's markings on a freshly captured half-track of the Panzer Lehr Division, 27 July 1944.

Above. Privates William Jackson and Joseph King wander around Caumont on a donkey, 8 July 1944. The town was liberated on 13 June by Company F of the 26th Infantry and the 742nd Tank Battalion.

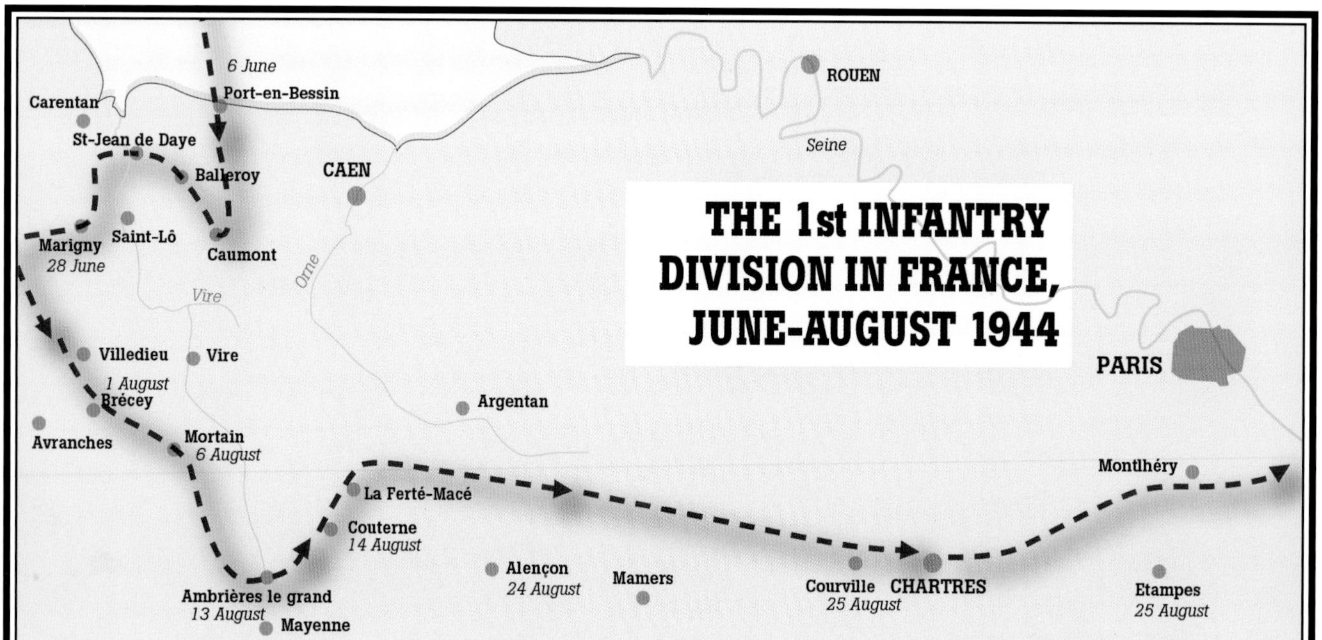

Above. A 57 mm anti-tank gun hidden in a sandbag bunker on a street corner in Caumont-l'Éventé.

Right. Big Red One dogfaces check over a Stug IV assault gun from the SS Division 'Das Reich'.

1st pushed towards the north to prevent the enemy movement. Relieved by the 30th Division, which would take the brunt of the imminent German counter-offensive, the "First Team" passed through Mayenne on 7 August. The Division was then ordered to head north towards Ferté-Macé. It often came up against isolated pockets of resistance. The rearguard of the Division at last managed to catch up at Bagnoles de l'Orne.

Towards the north

All of the Division's units began to move towards Chartres on 24 August. On the 25th, they gathered around Etampes, then advanced towards the river Seine which it crossed near Corbeil and Melun. The First Div. then drove hard towards northern France and Belgium, chasing the retreating Germans. On 31 August, the 1st was at Soissons where, a quarter of a century earlier, it had lost 9,000 men in four days of fighting. General Huebner as familiar with the region as, in 1918, he had commanded a 1st Division battalion there. In Soissons, the GI's discovered two railroad cars filled with food and for several days, their rations were improved with Westphalian sausage, noodles, tinned asparagus and cherries. Another surprise awaited them to the north-west of the town, the underground command center of Margival, deserted like the Mary Celeste. Moving away from Soissons, the Division crossed the Aisne and marched towards Laon and Maubeuge. The Fighting First regularly came across entire retreating German columns marching along the roads; cut off from all communication with their commanders, they were unaware that the Americans were chasing close behind. At each crossroads, lost Germans stumbled across American roadblocks and the chaos was even greater when these encounters took place at night. The Division took thousands of prisoners who were sent west, either on foot or crammed like sardines into 2.5-ton trucks. Less than four months after the Normandy landings, the Allies entered Belgium and, slowly but surely, moved closer to the borders of the Reich.

Below. 3 August 1944, a 1st Infantry Division patrol on the Mortain road.

Above.
3/16th Infantry soldiers take a ride on a Sherman of the 745th Tank Battalion, dashing through La Ferté-Macé, 14 August 1944.

Right.
An 18th Infantry GI checks the pockets of a German prisoner, looking for any documents that might be of use to the intelligence units.

Below.
The crossing of the Seine in the Corbeil sector, south of Paris, 24 August 1944.

Bottom, right.
1st Division soldiers guard a Luftwaffe pilot that they have just captured as he was escaping from his shot down plane.

WITH THE FIELD ARTILLERY

The writer and war correspondent AJ Liebling was reporting from Paris when the German invaded France in 1940. There after he covered the war for *The New Yorker*. In July 1944, he was embedded with the 1st Division's artillery.

"For this operation, I had decided to travel with Divarty- Divisional artillery headquarters battery. This was a battery without guns- as I need not explain for the artillerymen, but a lot of the infantrymen probably don't know yet. The headquarters battery merely had a switchboard, a set of maps, and a lot of telephone wires. Divarty was a small, travelling brain trust that moved quietly behind the front-line troops and called down fire on faraway Germans.

Divarty was under ordinary conditions an ideal place to follow the progress of a battle, or at least one division's part in it, because Divarty controlled the Piper Cubs that served as the Division's eyes. The pilots and observers were not Air Forces men but artillery officers. They reported not only on targets and the effect of the Division's artillery fire but on all enemy troop and vehicle movement they observed.

Every night during the offensive Divarty would set up its command post in a farmhouse or barn, black out the windows and chinks and lay its wire to the battalions, which laid wire to their batteries. Then, after nightfall, when the Cubs came down, the officers would sit around a long row of tables - in an atmosphere that used to make me think of a newspaper copy desk during the slack hours- drinking strong coffee and playing cribbage while they waited for telephone calls. A call would come in, officers would hold a short conversation, then remark, *"Infantry patrols report some sort of Jerry movement at that road junction at 4124. Mediums can reach it."* An officer would pick up the telephone again, make a call, and return to his cribbage game. Outside in the night the 155s would send a lot of high explosive screaming towards the dark crossroads.

I once asked General Andrus what chance there was of hitting anything useful with that kind of fire, and he said, *"About one in 50,000. But if they have inexperienced truck drivers it will scare them and slow them up some..."*

6 - Belgium and Germany

A half-track of the 3rd Battalion, 16th Infantry, enters the town of Mons, 2 September 1944.

On 1 September 1944, VII Corps found itself twenty kilometers from Belgium and the province of Hainaut. General Collins ordered all of its divisions to enter into the country the following day.

The 1st and 9th Infantry Divisions, supported by the 3rd Armored, operated together. The Big Red One advanced east towards Mons. The 16th Infantry penetrated into the town on 3 September, capturing 17,149 prisoners and more than 300 officers, including general Wahle of the 712. Infanterie-Division along with his entire staff, and colonel Hesse, an officer who was close to Rommel. At Bavai, a company of the 1/18th Infantry fought for five hours, killing 200 enemy soldiers and taking 460 prisoners and a large quantity of equipment. The 1st Infantry Division had covered more than 480 kilometers in a week and was temporarily cut-off from its supply lines. The GI's ate German rations and took gasoline from enemy vehicles.

The Division reached all of its objectives in the Namur region and by 8 September, the road to Liege was open.

German resistance was beginning to stiffen but the Wehrmacht was unable to buy enough time to set up an effective line of defense. On the 9th, the Fighting First crossed the Meuse river near Liège, then headed towards Herve in order to reach the German border, only encoun-

Two Fighting First infantrymen are seen here with members of the Belgian resistance just after the liberation of Mons.

Soldiers of the Aachen garrison, captured by the boys of the Big Red One on 15 October 1944.

Bottom, right.
Pte.V. Kamloz of the 26th Infantry looks at the reflection of his tired face in a shop window near Liege. Strangely, he has kept the assault vest that was issued for D-Day three months earlier.

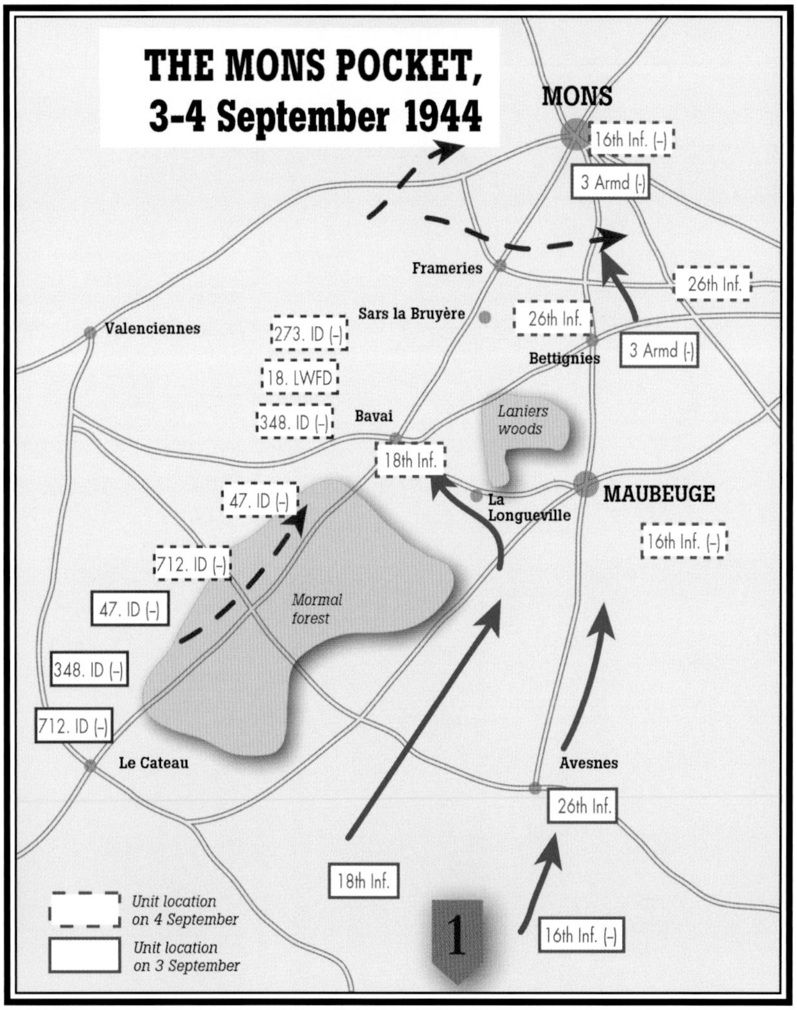

tering scattered rearguards. Thus, the division was the first American unit to break through the Siegfried Line on 12 September 1944. The men of HQ Company, 1/16th Infantry flew the American flag when crossing the border near Aachen.

The deployment of the Division's units this day took on an international flavour: a battalion was in Germany, one in Holland, the bulk of the Division in Belgium and its rear-echelon units still in France.

A Sherman M4 of Company C, 745th Tank Battalion, drives through a passageway under the Aachen-Rothe Erde railroad, 20 October 1944.

*Below.
Other Shermans of the 745th accompany the advance of the 2/26th Infantry.*

*Bottom.
Soldiers of the 3rd Bn./26th Infantry patrol in the northern suburbs of Aachen.*

A strengthened battalion even broke through the first line of defense six kilometers to the west of Aachen.

The Battle of Aachen

The fortress city of Aachen was strongly defended by 5,000 men under the command of Oberst (colonel) Gerhard Wilck. The American 30th Infantry Division attacked from the north, whereas the Big Red One went around the city via the east. It began the attack by an advance through a forest on 12 September. However,

ON THE SIEGRIED LINE

Mark S. Watson, a reporter for the *Baltimore Sun* daily paper, described how the Big Red One came upon the "Westwall":

"Surely, there was nobody in the Division, by that time, who had not heard of the Siegfried Line, but had finally decided with soldier's fatalism it could not be so much after all and certainly not enough to worry a Division which had battered its way across France and Belgium and even a corner of Holland. The talk of 'Dragon's teeth' did not terrify the boys at all.

However there was no rollicking laughter among us that day when we moved up over a ridge near Rotgen and, starting down into the low valley on the other side, came suddenly upon our first sight of the Line. There it lay - five rows of concrete blocks of uneven shapes and heights, close enough to each other to block a tank or tilt it off its tracks and expose it to fire from the concealed batteries on the distant slope.

Lengthwise the little valley the five rows reached, vanishing into a distant wood in one direction and over the horizon in the other.

Short of them, at first escaping the eye, was a very impressive tank obstacle.

Most fortunately for us, the line was not strongly held in this area. Thus, our engineers with great dispatch cleared the mine field, bulldozed a few tons of earth into one point of the great ditch and bridged the gap, and cleared the way for the American armor, followed by new waves of infantry and artillery."

during the course of the encirclement, the 16th Infantry came up against the Siegfried Line on the 15th. The attack was resumed on 8 October with the 18th Infantry pushing towards Verlautenheide and the 26th Infantry aiming at the heart of the city. As for the 16th Infantry, it held defensive positions in the Eilendorf sector. On 12 October, the 26th Infantry was solidly established in the industrial area between Aachen and Haaren. A determined attack was launched towards the city center the following day, supported by the 745th Tank Battalion. After heavy fighting, the high ground north of the town was captured, but fierce counter-attacks brought the advance to a brutal halt, also in the 16th Infantry sector. The fighting was intense for Crucifix Hill to the north-east and after only a few days, the 116th Infantry of the 29th Division was brought in to help the Big Red One that had already incurred over 2,000 casualties. The enemy was slowly pushed back into the town's suburbs. On 16 October, the Americans succeeded in completely encircling the town at Krefelder Straße. Following several days of intense street fighting, the remainder of the enemy garrison (300 men) laid down their arms. The battle resulted in 5,000 deaths on both sides and 5,600 German prisoners.

The Hürtgen Forest

On 26 October 1944, the First Army issued a statement saying that it appeared the enemy was growing in strength opposite VII Corps, especially in the dense Hürtgen Forest. Not wishing to bypass the thick woods and leave a strong enemy force to the rear, gen. Bradley decided to pinch the Germans out first. On 6 November, the 4th Infantry Division entered the forest; it was the first of several divisions to be suffer heavily there.

Relieved by the 104th Division, the Big Red One found itself, on 16 November, at the spearhead of the 1st Army offensive towards the Roer river to the east of Aachen. However, it was also forced to enter the dark Hürtgen For-

Top.
M10 Tank Destroyers of the 634th TD Battalion support the Division in the violent street fighting in Aachen.

Above. A soldier of the 26th Infantry guards German prisoners captured in the city.

Right.
In the town's ruins, a heavy MG team poses for a photo in an exposed position.

A German medic escorts wounded comrades in Aachen, guarded by a GI armed with a Thomson SMG.

est, that was chewing up GI's like mincemeat. Over the course of fifteen days, the Division fought tenaciously to gain less than 7 km of terrain. The bloody fighting around Hamich on 21-24 November would be one of the hardest battles of the war for the 16th Infantry. On 17 November, the unit was nearing Hill 232 that was being shelled by fifteen artillery battalions. It was at this time that the Germans counter-attacked in order to retake Hamich. The assault was supported by tanks, assault guns and strong artillery fire. Night and day the Germans attacked time and time again, and often were only stopped at the last moment when the regiment requested artillery concentrations on its own positions. The panzers were knocked out by planes and artillery, but also by the GIs themselves. One man, positioned in the upper floor of a house, succeeded in shooting a bazooka rocket into a tank's turret. At eleven o'clock, 1,300 8th Air Force bombers dropped their deadly loads in front of the Division's lines, followed at 14.25 hrs by the 9th Air Force, with the coup de grace being delivered at 15.00 hrs by a thousand four-engine RAF bombers! Fighting in the sector raged on until 8 pm. The 26th Infantry captured Laufenburg castle after a close-run fight with elements of the 47. Volksgrenadier-Division. Its 89th Regiment in particular, refused to give up and suffered very heavy losses due to its stubborn refusal to quit. The Germans withdrew slowly, hanging on to the high ground and making the most of the old castles that were scattered around the area. At the end of the month, the Germans brought into the line large rebuilt units. This was the case of the 3rd parachute division, fleshed out with very young recruits. But due to their lack of combat experience, they were terrified by the artillery barrages and surrendered in droves. However, in most cases, the enemy fought ferociously for each yard of ground in order to slow down the allied advance towards the Roer river. The 1st Division at last managed to reach the Merode sector but it was compelled to advance via a wooded area that was difficult for tanks and artillery units to move through. The Germans had the advantage of road access to the zone and they put this to good use.

On 29 November, a Fallschirmjäger battalion, supported by artillery and assault guns,

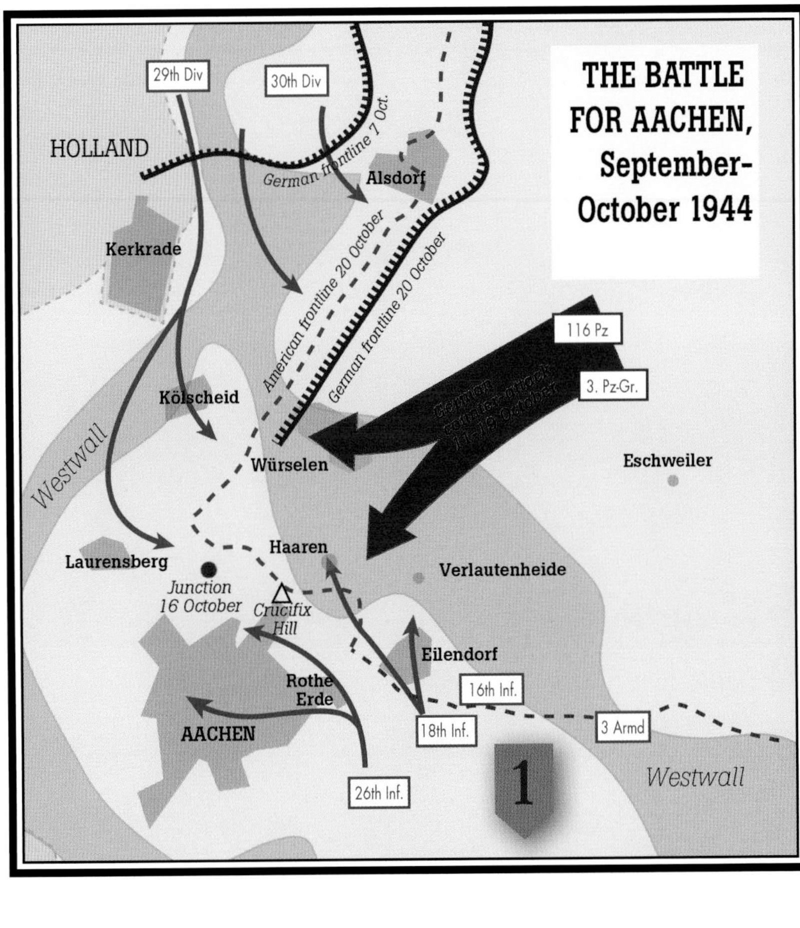

21 October 1944, Oberst Gerhard Wilck, commanding officer of the Aachen defenders, surrenders to the 1st Infantry Division.

16 September 1944, Aachen sector. Divisional engineers remove steel beams that have been buried as road blocks.

launched a powerful counter-attack at Merode. Two companies of the 26th Infantry, holding the village, were cut off and captured on 1 December 1944 after using up all of their ammunition. The terrible fighting in the Hürtgen Forest had bled these regiments dry and exhausted the battle hardened men of this prestigious unit. The 1st Division was at last relieved by the 9th Infantry Division on 5 December 1944 and left for a rest period in the Luchem-Langerwehe-Jüngersdorf-Merode sector, apart from the 16th Infantry, attached to V Corps. The respite only lasted a few days, the men only had time to eat decent meals, shower and receive a clean uniform before the Germans struck. For on 16 December 1944, they committed their last remaining forces in the West in Operation Nordwind in the Alsace, and by launching a major counter-offensive in the Belgian Ardennes. A victim of its reliability and reputation, the Big Red One was once again thrown into the cauldron.

More German prisoners gathered in the town. They seem, for the most part, very young.

This page. Company F men of the 16th Infantry move through the Hürtgen Forest, 18 November 1944. They are about to take part in the bloody fighting around Hamich; one of the toughest battles experienced by this unit throughout the entire war.

7 - The Battle of the Bulge

Above. Sergeant Ralph N. Nunn (from Knoxville, Tennessee), Company M/18th Infantry, waits for German paratroopers to emerge from Sourbrodt wood.

Below. Late in December 1944, the 26th Infantry anti-tank company sets up a 57mm gun.

The Division was quickly sent to the Malmédy sector. Throughout the night of 16-17 December, the 26th Infantry covered more than fifty kilometers by truck in freezing weather to Elsenborn camp.

Below. A 1st Division jeep driver has made himself an impressive-looking head warmer out of a wool blanket. Ardennes, 14 December 1944.

Right.
Men of Company I, 16th Infantry, ride on a Sherman during the attack on Schoppen, 15 January 1945.

This abandoned Belgian army training ground was nothing more than a collection of derelict buildings without windows and doors. On the 17th at 15.30 hrs, the 18th Infantry was taken by 2.5-ton GMC trucks towards Eupen in order to establish defensive positions around the eastern perimeter of the town.

Under the direct orders of V Corps, their mission was to organize and coordinate the defenses and block the roads leading to Monschau and Malmédy. A force of approximately 500 German paratroopers was reported in various parts of the woods south of Eupen. On 18 December, the 16th Infantry moved out of the

Below. 31 December 1944, Private Paul Romanick of Battery B, 103rd Anti-aircraft Battalion, attached to the 1st Division, cleans a snow-covered 40mm anti-aircraft gun in the Sourbrodt sector.

Right.
3rd Bn./26th Infantry dogfaces look at a German air-dropped container at Bullingen, 1 January 1945.

Above. Weywertz, January 1945, a Weasel of the 3rd Battalion, 16th Infantry, carries wounded men to an aid post.

Right.
A platoon from Company C, 16th Infantry, move off towards Faymonville during the allied counter-offensive in the Belgian Ardennes, 16 January 1945. The white camouflage smocks have been made in France and Belgium by local manpower.

Below.
A captured German halftrack that has been put back in to service by Company L of the 16th Infantry, near Schoppen, 22 January 1945.

American forces rest area near Verviers and Herve in order to take up positions near Robertville with the task of defending the southwest sector. Patrols made contact with adjacent units and the battalions remained on high alert. On the northern shoulder of the salient, the 1st Division veterans held the line with the 2nd and 99th Infantry Divisions. On Elsenborn ridge, their resistance forced general Model to alter the plans for the 6. Panzerarmee. The regiments of the Big Red One would face three divisions, the 12th SS panzer, 3rd parachute and 12th Volksgrenadier Divisions. Despite its exhaustion after almost six months of endless fighting, the 1st established a defensive perimeter all around the small town of Bütgenbach, a vital road junction. On 20 December, the 3rd Battalion, 16th Infantry, repulsed several probing attacks. The 2nd Battalion held

Top right.
A Sherman M4 supports the 16th Infantry during the capture of Amel in the pinching out phase of the Battle of the Bulge, 25 January 1945.

Above.
A 1st Division anti-tank unit half-track in the Bütgenbach sector. The 57mm gun proved to be efficient against the panzers when used by a determined crew.

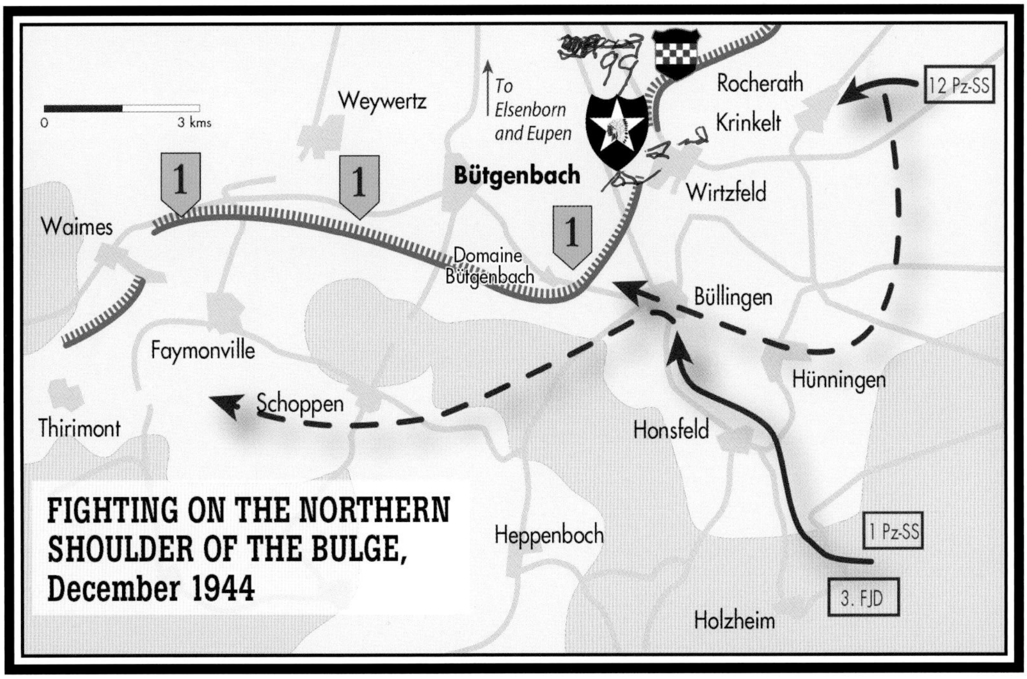

Above.
January 1945. In a landscape covered by thick snow, a 26th Infantry machine-gunner guards a road that was recaptured a short while before by his unit.

Right. 16th Infantry men check abandoned buildings looking for possible Wehrmacht stragglers in the Schoppen sector.

Below.
Schoppen sector, 16th Infantry soldiers climb into an M29 Weasel tracked carrier. In the background we can see a Tank Destroyer of the 634th Battalion.

Waimes and fought off several attempts by the enemy to push through. The 1st Battalion was held in reserve. The 18th Infantry was sent to Sourbrodt, where it was held in reserve until further notice. The regimental commander decided, however, to send the 2nd Battalion to the 26th Infantry sector to bolster their first and second battalions. By the evening, Company I of the 18th Infantry had set up a roadblock south of Sourbrodt. The following day, the

BITTER FIGHTING AT BÜTGENBACH

Iris Carpenter, a British journalist for the *Boston Globe*, reports on the battle near Bütgenbach:

"On the morning of the 20th (December) tanks came again with the dawn. They ran systematically up and down our foxholes, then went on down the Bütgenbach road right to the (26th Infantry's) 2nd Battalion CP. This command post was a farm which had been used as a hospital and abandoned in a hurry... such a hurry that the nurses had left some of their clothes behind.

Commanding 2nd Battalion CP was Lt. Colonel Derrill M. Daniel (...) who looked upon that particular morning to see three German tanks positioned within fifty yards of him. He dispassionately rounded up the clerks and cooks, drivers and medics who comprised his staff; armed them, posted them and told them to "hold fast". They did though the tanks got close enough, as one of the cooks said "To ram its bastard gun through the windows."

Communications with the Division were out, so Daniel sent messengers to ask for "all the fire you can throw in the backyard".

A sergeant, whose name unhappily (...) does not appear in my notes, decided that it was high time that something was done about the lead tank. He had never, until that morning fought anything tougher than an index file; but he took a bazooka and a couple of drivers, made his way out of the farmhouse and around the back of the tank and knocked it out. The other two tanks withdrew and Division received the laconic message "*Attack repulsed, send litters.*"

In the two top photos, a German medic, captured in the 1st Infantry Division sector, is taken to the regimental aid station in Mürringen (to the west of Büllingen), so that he can give first aid to the wounded of both sides.

Above. Pfc Cox of Company M of the 26th Infantry, equipped with a snow camouflage smock, carefully enters the ruins of Mürringen. January 1945.

2nd Battalion, 16th Infantry pushed its lines as far as the positions held by the 1st Battalion without encountering any difficulties. The 3rd Battalion repulsed numerous aggressive patrols and deep mine fields were laid in front of its positions. However, on the morning of the 22nd, south of Bütgenbach, some of the 26th Infantry combat positions were penetrated by enemy tanks and infantry. At 09.55 hrs, the 1st Bn./18th Infantry was sent to the area by truck and launched a counter-attack in the south-east in order to recover the lost ground.

More mines and barbed wire

In the evening, the command post of the 18th Infantry moved to Nidrum, a small village north of Bütgenbach. On the 23rd, Co. F of the 16th Infantry moved its positions to high ground. Its battalions strengthened their defenses and laid more mines, as well as new barbed wire entanglements. A new enemy penetration was halted by the 3rd Battalion. Mid-morning, the 2/18th Infantry regrouped and organized the entire defense of the south-west sector of Bütgenbach; the regiment held the whole area south of the town. The 3/18th was placed in reserve on the northern outskirts of Nidrum,

Right.
Sergeant N.T. Kimball, Battery B, 5th Field Artillery Battalion, examines a German 37mm anti-tank gun, abandoned on a roadside near Mürringen.

Far right. The Bütgenbach sector, 18th Infantry men check the road for possible booby-traps left behind by the withdrawing Germans.

Left.
Faymonville, on the Bütgenbach-Waimes road, two 16th Infantry GIs take a look at an armored car that had been captured by the Germans.

Bottom.
Men of the 3rd Battalion, 26th Infantry, head to the front-line, passing by a lined up column of vehicles in Mürringen, 31 January 1945.

whereas the two front-line battalions actively patrolled in the south, making contact with scattered enemy groups in the Bütgenbacher Heck sector. The supply trains were sent to the Elsenborn camp north of Nidrum. The 3rd Battalion carried out patrols in order to try and detect any enemy attack. The minefields and barbed wire defenses were strengthened on Christmas Eve. The 2/16th repulsed an infantry attack supported by panzers. For almost two weeks, the 26th Infantry held its positions in the face of repeated attacks. Its rifle companies were understrength and 90% of the men were green replacements. The second battalion only had seven officers left that had been on its rolls before 1 December 1944. This unit had the hardest task as it was at the forefront at Domaine Bütgenbach, by the Malmédy road, essential to the success of the German breakthrough. Its flank was also exposed to attacks coming from Büllingen.

The Division's lines were briefly broken through at Bütgenbach, but the GI's finally repulsed the Waffen-SS tanks and infantry. On 25 December, Co. K of the 16th Infantry relieved Co. L, the latter having suffered heavy casualties in repulsing a strong infantry attack. On the 26th, the 2nd Battalion once again fought off a fresh attack. The next day patrols were sent out around Faymonville. On 29 December, the 16th Infantry sent strong patrols out to make contact with the enemy. Heavy artillery barrages rained down on the American positions, causing heavy damage to the defenses. By the 30th, the positions had been greatly improved and several German outposts eliminated. On the last day of 1944, Co. L of the 16th Infantry relieved Co. I, which was placed in reserve at Weywertz.

On 15 January, the Big Red One went back on the offensive, conquering Steinbach in order to open a passage towards St. Vith for the 7th Armored Division. It was slowed down by stiff resistance to the north-east of Schoppen, whilst at the same time the 16th Infantry mopped up Bambusch wood. On 28 January, the Division approached once more the Siegfried Line, advancing through the Buchholz woods.

The Siegfried line, again!

On 2 February, the GIs broke through the Westwall for a second time, although in this instance it was fiercely defended. They crossed two rows of 'dragon's teeth' in spite of a huge amount of anti-personnel and tank mines. After Scheitert and Ramsheid, the Division captured the Hollerath road hub on 3 February. After eliminating the last concrete strong-points on the town's high ground, the Division was relieved by the 99th Infantry Division on 5 February and assembled the following day in the

Top left.
31 January 1945 in the Mürringen sector, Company L, 3rd Bn., 26th Infantry, moves up to the front-line through a thick fog.

Above. Nidrum in the Bütgenbach sector. This 1st Division GI carries out the vital daily task of cleaning his Garand M1 rifle.

Left.
23 January 1945, Sourbordt. General Huebner awards the DSC to lieutenants Howard MacConchie, John Synowsky and Pfc Harry Griffin. All three won this medal in Normandy.

Bottom.
1st Combat Engineers repair a road necessary for pinching out the Ardennes bulge.

vicinity of Aywaille, near Liège. The cost of the Battle of the Bulge was very heavy: the Division had lost 458 men killed between 17 December 1944 and 7 February 1945. However, in 21 days it had taken two thousand prisoners.

8 - To Czechoslovakia and Victory in Europe

Opposite.
A division MP tries to get as much protection from the rain as he can on the edge of Hürtgen Forest.

Bottom.
Engineers prepare to clear roads that have turned to mud after the thaw at Langenbroich, close to Hürtgen Forest.

The Division returned to the front-line in Germany in the Grosshau sector, west of the Roer river, on 8 February 1945.

When the Allies reached its banks in December 1944 it made for a formidable obstacle as it was wide and fast flowing as well as being well-defended. The 1st took over the 8th Infantry lines for a month and on 25 February, crossed the Roer at Kreuzau. Despite their heavy defeats in the Ardennes and against the Russians, the Wehrmacht put up its usual ferocious resistance. The division, however, advanced, often at night in leaps and bounds towards the Rhine. In this way, the Germans were unable to re-establish their defensive positions each evening when the fighting died down. They were forced to withdraw rapidly and fight rearguard actions in urban areas. Flak units positioned in front of the Ruhr area to defend it against bomber raids, resisted fanatically with their 20mm guns in a ground role.

On 1 March, the 16th Infantry crossed the Neffel, heralding the offensive towards Bonn and Rhineland. A bridgehead was established on the far bank of the Erft on 3 March.

Above.
General Andrus accompanies Omar Bradley, commander of the American 12th Army Group, to the divisional CP in Hürtgen Forest, February 1945.

Far right.
2 February, near Kreuzau. Pte. Michael Swinkin, Company B, 16th Infantry, awaits the order for his battalion to cross the Roer river.

Right.
14 February 1945, T/5 Bertel C. Swanberg, of the 1st Engineer Combat Battalion, receives the Distinguished Service Cross from Brigadier General George A. Taylor (second in command - 1st infantry Division). Swanberg was decorated for his actions against the enemy on 14 November 1944.

The capture of Bonn

7 March 1945 was the 387th day of combat for the Fighting First when it faced Bonn. The same day, 726 prisoners were taken, bringing the total up to 60,000 so far throughout the war. Bonn was a vital military objective. Built on the banks of the Rhine, it opened the way towards to the west of the Reich. Since January, it had been given 'fortress' status and the German troops had been ordered to hold it to the last man. The defenders, however, were taken by surprise; they had been expecting a large-scale attack with aerial bombardments and heavy artillery barrages, but the Americans had advanced stealthily. The decisive penetration was carried out by the 16th Infantry along the river towards the south in the early hours of 8 March. By the end of the afternoon, two 26th Infantry battalions were in the streets. Contact was maintained thanks to the 14th Cavalry Group along with the 8th Infantry Division in the north. The 3rd Armored Division

Right.
15 February 1945, a 16th Infantry half-track churns up a muddy road in the Hürtgen Forest.

Right.
Two 1st Division GI's look at the slogan "Sieg oder Chaos" (victory or chaos), painted on a farm gate.

Bottom.
19 February 1945, Lieutenant-Colonel HG Leonard, commanding the 18th Infantry, shows his company commanders the attack plans beyond the Roer river in view of establishing a bridgehead outside of Vicht.

Bottom, right.
25 February 1945, Company B, 16th Infantry, nears Schneidhausen in order to cross the Roer.

Below, right. An M1919A4 light machine-gun team prepares to cover the advance towards Vicht.

BLACK GI'S WITH THE BIG RED ONE

Owing the severe shortage of Infantry replacements after the battle of the Bulge, on 11 March, three platoons of black enlisted men were assigned to the division as ordered by the 1st Army.

The American high command had abolished the taboo of segregation in its ranks, which meant that Black soldiers were massively assigned to support units, and in some fighting units (engineers, artillery, armor) led by mostly white officers.

These soldiers caught up with the division at Bonn, and made up the 4th Platoon of B Company in the both the 16th and 18th Infantry, and in Co. K of the 26th. For the first time in history, African-American soldiers wore the Big Red One patch.

Other commanding generals among the less obtuse, including Terry Allen and its 104th Division, successfully integrated Black GI's, sometimes even as individual replacements in white rifle squads.

Above.
Company B, 16th Infantry crossing the Roer on a pontoon in the Kreuzau sector, 25 February 1945.

Below.
Men of the Fighting First crossing the Roer on a light pontoon bridge.

joined its forces with those of the 1st Division. At 21.00 hrs, the main bridge over the Rhine, which offered escape from the allied pressure, was blown by the German officer in charge of the demolition charges. Resistance gradually decreased. The end came in the town center on the morning of the next day. The under-equipped and hungry defenders, most of whom were young recruits who had only just finished basic training in Denmark, surrendered en masse. Intense street fighting continued in the western suburbs but the German resistance to the west of the Rhine collapsed.

Widening the Remagen bridgehead

The Big Red One continued towards the Rhine, fighting from village to village, finding in its path the 29. Panzer-Grenadier Regiment, then the paratroopers of the 5. Fallschirm-jäger-Regiment, who launched determined counter-attacks. With the support of the 3rd Armored Division, the Division's task was to widen the Remagen bridgehead. Faced with this serious threat, the enemy brought in the 363. Infanterie-Division, as well as the 244 and 902. Sturmgeschutz-Brigades, armed with assault guns.

On 24 March, VII Corps orders stipulated that the Division had to take part in eliminating enemy forces south of the Sieg river. The spearhead was formed by the 3rd Armored Division, followed by the 1st on its left and Terry Allen's 104th Infantry Division on its right. During the day, it appeared that the Americans had struck at the right time, just before the enemy was about to launch a strong counter-attack. The fighting for Uckerath, held by the 62. Volksgrenadier Div. and the 363. ID, was extremely violent. With their larger units under pressure, the Germans began to transfer them to the northern bank of the Sieg. On 30 March, the Big Red One attacked with three regiments along the high ground overlooking the town of Siegen north of the river. On Easter Sunday, 1

Above.
1st Division GIs rest on heathland near Soller, late February 1945.

Below.
Ready to cross the Rhine, a heavily-laden soldier of the 16th Infantry, awaits the order to move off.

THE LIBERATION OF THE DEATH CAMPS

On 8 May 1945, units of the Big Red One and the 9th Armored Division reached Zwodau and Falkenau an der Eger, two satellites of the larger death camp at Flossenbürg in Bavaria, that had been previously liberated by the 90th Division. Both camps were located in what is now the Czech republic. Zwodau had been established by the SS for aircraft construction and housed about 1,200 deportees, while a mere 60 survivors remained at Falkenau. The 1st Infantry Division scavenged in the area to feed them and provided medical care.

On May 9, captain Richmond Kimble, corporal Samuel Fuller's battalion commander in the 16th Infantry, asked him to shoot in 16 mm black and white film (with the movie camera his mother had gifted him), a testimony of the Falkenau camp. The officer wanted the full horror of the place to be recorded, such as stacks of corpses awaiting burial in mass graves.

The footage was not released until 1988, when it was featured with Fuller's approval in a French documentary, *Falkenau, vision de l'impossible*. Certain scenes has inspired the final minutes of his movie *The Big Red One*.

A still of Fuller in the USA before leaving for overseas, using the 16-mm movie camera his mother had given him.

April, the 8th Infantry Division relieved the 1st. The town fell two days later.

The Ruhr Pocket

The 1st Division was then transported by truck over almost 250 kilometers to the east, to positions in the Buren sector south-west of Paderborn, a town that had been heavily damaged by air raids. This mission, the closing of the Ruhr Pocket, saw the longest tactical move undertaken by the Big Red One. On 1 April 1945, the Division advanced towards the north in order to carry out the linking up of the 1st and 9th Armies, thus closing the pocket. It was then ordered to move, still accompanied by the VII Corps 3rd Armored and 104th Infantry Divisions, towards the north-east. After crossing the Weser, the Division had to head towards Osterode on the western edge of the Harz mountains. On 8 April 1945, it found it-

28 February at Vettweiss. Making the most of a halt during their advance, these soldiers of Company G, 16th Infantry, take some rest outside a building. The half-track on the left, towing a 57mm gun, belongs to the regimental anti-tank company. The round tactical marking near the vehicle's nickname "Public Zoo" is visible on the side.

self on the banks of the Weser river with the 3rd Armored, but all the crossings had been destroyed. The 16th and 18th Infantry established a bridgehead, whilst the 26th Infantry, transported by trucks, attacked towards Einbeck. The opposing forces comprised entirely of training units and a few Waffen-SS elements. Indeed, the Paderborn area was home to numerous German army training grounds. With the 4th Cavalry Group on its northern flank, the Fighting First was tasked with combing through the edges of the Harz Mountains without entering them, then to continue as quickly as possi-

Two photographs taken during the crossing of the Roer. The GI taking aim with his Garand rifle has attached a chemical grenade to his webbing.

ble to the Elbe.

Into the mountains dark…

Allied intelligence feared that the Harz Mountains would become a redoubt where the enemy could regroup and rebuild its withdrawing units. The terrain obviously favoured the defender with a fragmented road network and dense forests, intersected by ravines.

The Americans were slowed down by roadblocks and destroyed bridges. At Osterode, on 11 April, fierce fighting took place with some heavy tanks of the 507. schwere Panzer-Abteilung, whose workshops were in the town.

On 14 April, the 16th Infantry experienced tough fighting for St. Andreasberg, defended by panzers, assault guns and infantry, positioned on the high ground. However, the scattered and overrun German troops began surrendering from 19 April onwards. The following day, the Harz sector was totally conquered. On 30 April, the 1st Infantry Division was trans-

Top, left.
In Weilerwist, Michael C. DiCarlo of Company H, 16th Infantry, use a wheelbarrow to carry heavy 81mm mortar projectiles to the mortar positioned in a neighboring field.

Above. The 18th Infantry continues its advance through Frauwüllesheim, near Düren, Westphalia, 29 February 1945.

Left.
5 March 1945, men of the 80th Chemical Mortar Battalion set up their mortars in Weilerwist, in support of the impending 2nd Bn./16th Infantry attack on Metternich.

Right.
A 105mm gun of the 26th Infantry Cannon Company, opens fire on enemy positions in the woods near Bliesheim on 5 March.

Below.
Company I of the 26th Infantry in Bliesheim, 5 March 1945. The Sherman tank, armed with a 76mm gun, probably belongs to the 745th Tank Battalion.

Below, right. These 26th Infantry dogfaces look for enemy activity in the woods around the village.

ferred to V Corps.

The very day Adolf Hitler was committing suicide in besieged Berlin, the 1st Division was relieved by the 97th Infantry Division. It then received orders to move towards the Czech border.

In Czechoslovakia

In its first days in Czechoslovakia, up to 2 May 1945, the Division was to the east of Asch and Cheb. Here, its positions were consolidated, patrols sent out and only local attacks made. Cheb (Eger in German) was in the Sudeten region annexed by the Reich in 1938.

The 26th Infantry had its 2nd and 3rd Battalions up front with the 1st in reserve. In the center of the area, the 16th Infantry kept its 1st and 2nd Battalions in Czechoslovakia with the 3rd Battalion in reserve at Selb. The 18th Infantry was on the right flank. On 5 May, the Division advanced 14 kilometers towards Karlsbad (today known as Karlowy Vary), along a 48 kilometer-wide front, experiencing very tough fighting in the mountainous regions of Cheb.

Right.
The flag that the 5th Field Artillery flew when crossing the Rhine in December 1918 is handed over to a battalion officer prior to repeating the operation in March 1945.

Below.
March 1945, Barnheim. This 7th Field Artillery gun crew loads its 200,000th shell of the war.

The 1st and 2nd Battalions of the 18th Infantry were in a position to reach their objectives, but the 3rd Bn. came up against a more determined resistance until the early hours of 6 May. Several well-defended roadblocks were rapidly pushed aside. Company B of the 745th Tank Battalion and 18th Infantry soldiers attacked a group of Germans dug-in along the high ground north of Drenica. Casualties were light, one officer and 23 men wounded. In the early hours of 6 May, the 9th Armored Division advanced through the forward positions held by the Big Red One and attacked eastwards. In several places, the Germans put up a stiff fight with anti-tank guns and infantry. To the east of Drenica, the defenders held on tenaciously until the intervention of armor and Tank Destroyers. The 16th Infantry attack was preceded by artillery preparation. The 7th Field Artillery Battalion moved twice moved closer to the front in order to provide immediate support. In the early

Below, left. 16th Infantry soldiers mop up the town of Bonn and its last pockets of resistance.

Below. Bonn, 9 March 1945, two Big Red One soldiers look for movement in the street leading to the bridge over the Rhine. This fighting is considered as being the Regiment's most successful action.

Above. 1st Division soldiers advancing in Bonn. The Americans found more than 200 deserters in the cellars of the town who had chosen to await the invaders.

Right. A 1st Infantry Division GI guards a crossroads in the streets of Bonn.

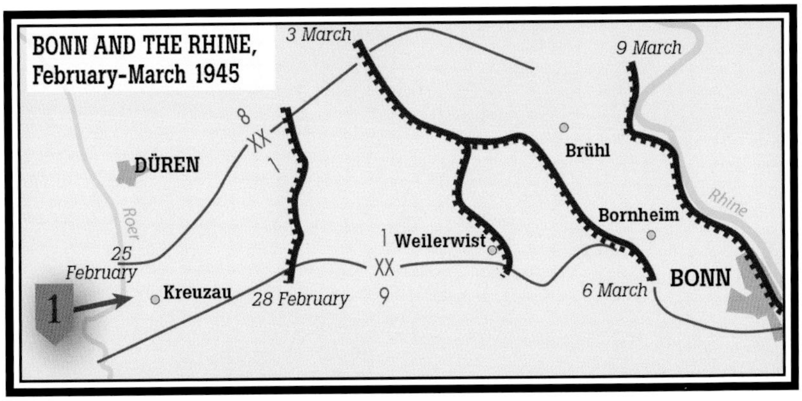

hours of 7 May 1945, the 1st Division units and those of the 9th Armored were continuing their advance east when they received the order to halt and remain where they were. The Big Red One command then received General Eisenhower's official message notifying them of the unconditional surrender of German forces that very morning.

The German officers of the XII army corps in the region gave themselves up to the 1st Division. General Herbert Osterkamp signed the act of surrender along with the Division's second in command, Brigadier General George A. Taylor. Throughout his interrogation, Osterkamp revealed that his army corps had no more than approximately 2,200 soldiers left within his

Top right.
Private James R. Kennedy (from Jacksonville, Florida) received a light head wound from a sniper a few moments before this photo was taken in the Sharfenberg sector on 2 April.

Above.
8 April 1945, the 16th Infantry cross the Weser in assault boats, following the capture of Wehrden, and prepare to advance towards Furstenberg.

three exhausted divisions.

After VE-Day

After the surrender, the 1st Infantry Division was tasked with manning roadblocks, checkpoints and guarding prisoner of war camps. With the mass arrival of soldiers fleeing the Red Army, a huge concentration zone was set up to take them in near Cheb. The Division remained in north-western Czechoslovakia for a month after VE Day. It was relieved by the 79th Division early in June and departed for Gunzenhausen in Germany. A memorial on the outskirts of Cheb remembers the 775 men of the Fighting First who lost their lives between February and 8 May 1945.

When the Second World War came to an end, the Division had lost a total of 21,023 men (killed, wounded and missing) out of the 43,743 soldiers who had served in its ranks since its creation. It had undertaken three landings (North Africa, Sicily and Normandy) and its soldiers had won a total of 20,752 medals and awards, including 16 Medals of Honor. It had taken 188,832 enemy prisoners during the course of 443 days of combat. Its HQ had been set up in 101 different locations throughout western Europe.

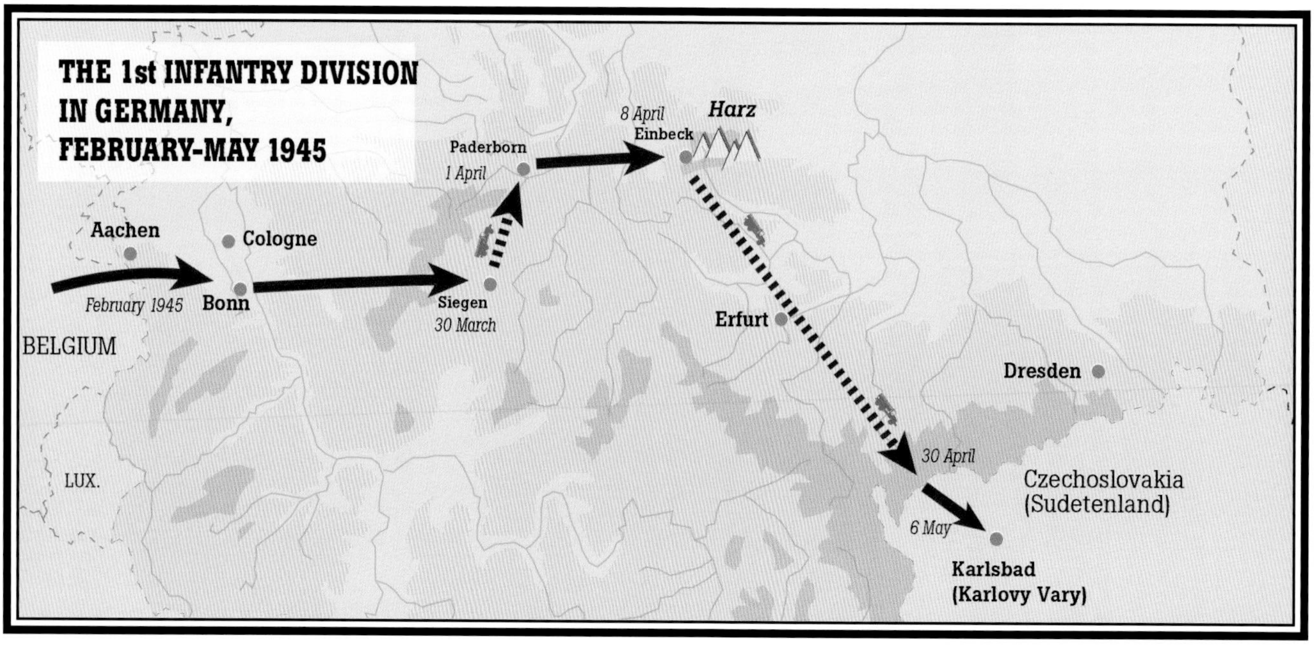

Below.
Prisoners captured by the Division in Dorste, Lower Saxony on 11 March 1945. Their being placed against the wall is perhaps explained by the fact that they are SS panzer troops. The GIs in the photo are, from left to right, Sergeant Joseph F. Mannix (from Tarentum, Pennsylvania) and Private Herbert Lusk (from Demberton, Virginia), both of Company A, 16th Infantry.

Above. Fierce fighting took place in Sankt Andreasberg in the Harz region on 14 April 1945. Sherman M4A3 tanks of the 745th Tank Battalion are positioned in the street to assist in the flushing out of snipers.

Above.
In this strange photo, taken on 10 April 1945, soldiers of Company K, 16th Infantry, grab some sleep on a road whilst waiting for the tanks to catch up before resuming their advance.

Above.
Sergeants Mallory J. Jacopine and Worner W. Kahl, of the divisional Military Police, with the 100,000th German soldier captured by the Division, Harz Mountains, 23 April 1945.

Right. Lieutenant Art Staymates (right) of Co. B, 26th Infantry, accompanied by one of his men, search a very young soldier captured during the last days of the war in Germany.

Below.
Brigadier General George A. Taylor, the assistant division commander, receives the surrender of general Fritz Benicke at Elbogen (Loket in Czechoslovakia) 7 May 1945. "Division Benicke" was a thorn in the Americans' side at the beginning of May; most of its personnel was made up of officer cadets who were training in the Sudetenland.

9 - Occupation and the Cold War

Right.
A souvenir Big Red One bracelet made in Germany. (M. Pascal Collection)

Far right.
A 1st Division Private First Class stands guard outside an official building in Germany. Note the white equipment and chromed helmet.

Below.
A metal token, usually bearing a service number, used as pass for 2/16th Infantry personnel. This battalion was based at Salzburg, Austria in 1945. Made by Lauer in Nuremberg. (P. Coleman collection)

Following the victory in Europe, the Fighting First found itself part of the occupation forces in Germany for the second time since 1918.

Despite the mass demobilization after the victory against Japan, the division received sufficient drafts to enable it to carry out its role in Europe, where it remained without interruption until 1955.

As seen on the map below, in 1945 it spread out its units across the entire American Occupation zone, as well as in Vienna and the Bremen enclave. Its HQ was established at Bad Tölz near Munich. The 16th Infantry battalions were in Vienna, Salzburg and Berlin. The 18th Infantry was shared out between Bremen and Frankfurt and finally, the 26th Infantry was garrisoned at Ludwigsburg, Munich and Nuremberg. The 16th Infantry, commanded by Colonel John P. Evans, would create a platoon of men especially chosen for ceremonial duties. They provided the guard for HQs and also security personnel for the war crimes trials at Nuremberg. As a reward for services

Bottom, left. 26th Infantry men in full dress guarding some of the accused (including Goering and Hess in the first row) at the Nuremberg trials.

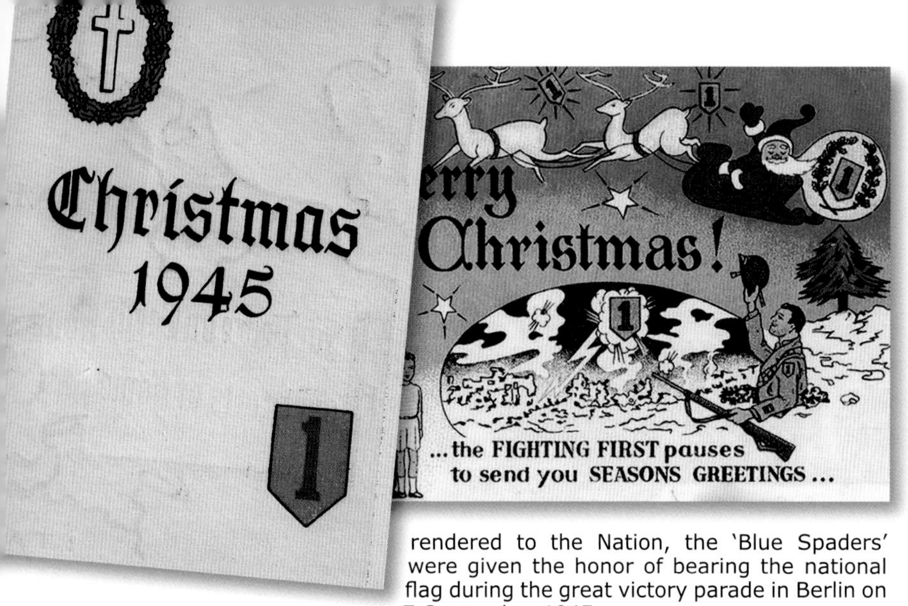

rendered to the Nation, the 'Blue Spaders' were given the honor of bearing the national flag during the great victory parade in Berlin on 7 September 1945.

Up until the nineteen-fifties, the American occupation forces in Germany (290,000 men in 1946) were made up of the 1st Division, a separate infantry battalion and a mobile law and order unit, the Constabulary, formed with ten mechanized cavalry regiments.

Above. A Christmas card printed for 1st Division soldiers in 1945.

Top, right. 26th Infantry GIs in 1949.

Below. 26th Infantry souvenir album published in Germany in 1949. The division was commanded by General Frank Milburn, the former XXI Corps commander from 1943-45.
(A. Basso collection)

Bottom
A long serving NCO is photographed in front of the 3rd Battalion/16th Infantry HQ in Berlin.

The Cold War

However, at the end of 1946, the lack of personnel and the wide spread of the garrisons, meant that the Division was only at 20% combat efficiency. In 1947, it became an operational reserve unit and a rapid reaction force in support of the Constabulary. With its units brought together in the Grafenwöhr training grounds near Nuremberg, it underwent training for this role. Following the 1948 reorganization, it received a draft of 5,000 men. Given the threat from Eastern Europe and the creation of NATO, the Division became a component of the West's rampart in Germany. Many exercises were held to train for the eventuality of a Warsaw Pact forces invasion. In August 1950, the Division was at full strength. From 1951 onwards, it was joined by other units shipped to Europe to become part of the new 7th Army that was reactivated in Germany. In August, it became part of V Corps, along with the 4th Infantry and 2nd Armored Divisions. Like the other large units, it was handicapped by the fragmentation of its units in several widespread garrisons, and by the difficulty in finding local training grounds. At this time it was under the command of Major General. Thomas S. Timberman, the only V Corps general without combat experience in Europe during the world war. Finally, in 1955, during the course of Operation Gyroscope, the Division was replaced in Germany by the 10th Infantry Division from Fort Riley, Kansas. After thirteen years overseas, the Division was given a rapturous welcome and great parade in the streets of New York. It was then reorganized on the flexible lines of the 'Pentomic' type division, in order to operate on a battlefield placed under the threat of the atomic weapon. With the introduction of peacetime compulsory military service (the "draft") during the Cold War, the Big Red One provided basic training for new recruits in America.

10 - The Big Red One in movies

The best-known movie about the division is without a doubt Samuel Fuller's 'The Big Red One'. This famous film noir director was himself a WW2 veteran of the unit. Initially shown in its 113 minute format, the movie was later modified with the addition of cut scenes and now lasts 162 minutes.

The cast:
- Lee Marvin: Sergeant Possum
- Mark Hamill: Griff, the soldier who did not want to kill
- Robert Carradine: Zab
- Bobby di Cicco: Vinci
- Kelly Ward: Johnson
- Siegfried Rauch: Schroeder

It should be noted that Mark Hamill was already famous for his role as Luke Skywalker in *Star Wars*. John Wayne was supposed to play the role of Sergeant Possum, but Fuller chose Lee Marvin, a Marine Corps veteran, instead. The storyline goes as follows: it is November 1918, Sergeant Possum sees a tired-looking German soldier appear and does not understand what he is saying. Unsure as to the German's intentions, he shoots him dead only to learn after that the unfortunate soldier was announcing the end of the war. Then, during a short scene, the sergeant mentions the idea of a divisional patch with a large red One, using a piece of German uniform. Twenty-four years later, Sergeant Possum takes part in the landings in North Africa, with the same division and leading a rifle squad made up of young recruits, including Privates Zab, Vinci, Johnson and Griff. The movie then follows these men from Sicily, France and the Normandy Landings and ends in Czechoslovakia in 1945. The movie was shot in Ireland and Israel; the short scene of a patrol in the snow-covered Ardennes was shot in Central Park, New York! The movie was started in 1978 and carried on into the following year, appearing at cinemas in France on 28 May. The movie was part of the official selection at the Cannes Festival the same year and won the Palme d'or. Fuller, who had worked on the project for twenty years, came up with the scenario by studying the notebooks that he had kept when he was a GI with the 18th Infantry. The movie is in the first person and the narrator, Private Zab, chews on a cigar as Fuller did. The GI is not glorified, there is no heroic or melodramatic side to the story concerning his sacrifice unlike so many other movies. Rather, the GI is seen as just a man who is trying to survive; also, the German soldier is not portrayed as a diabolical enemy, but rather a professional soldier, symbolized by the indestructible Schroeder. The director also cleverly chose not to shoot only battle scenes,

but also all of the small day to day aspects that made up the life of a soldier. The entire approach of the movie is summed up in its epilogue: "*Surviving is the only glory in war*". There are several memorable scenes, such as the one in Sicily where a child attempts to bury the corpse of one of his parents, the fighting in a psychiatric hospital, the mother giving birth in a tank or one of the final scenes with the dying child at the Falkenau camp which humanizes the sergeant. There are also fleeting, funny or symbolic scenes such as the rabbits that run when the soldiers retreat, the roll of toilet paper that explodes during the landings in France, or the Hitler Youth kid, too young to be shot, but who is spanked for killing an American soldier! The attention to uniform detail is relatively good for a movie of this period, both American and German, and we see the changes to the uniforms throughout the campaigns. As is the case with many contemporary movies, the panzers are post-war tanks, in this case vaguely modified Israeli Super Shermans. It is also ironical that the Afrika Korps soldiers in the El Guettar battle scene are played by Israeli soldiers!

II - From Vietnam to the Gulf

The 1st Infantry Division has been stationed in the USA at Fort Riley (Kansas) since 1955.

Right.
South of the Cambodian border, 2 April 1967. Following a firefight in the jungle, 1st Battalion/26th Infantry wounded receive first aid before being evacuated by helicopter.
(US Army)

During the crisis of 1962-1963, caused by the building of the Berlin Wall, four divisional Battle Groups were rotated in the American West Berlin zone. At the same time, 3rd Brigade elements were garrisoned in the Stuttgart region.

Vietnam, 1965-1970

The Big Red One arrived in south-east Asia in July 1965. At the end of the year it took part in three large operations: Hump, Bushmaster one and Bushmaster two. In 1966, it took part in Operations Marauder, Crimp II and Rolling Stone and in the battles of Ap Tau O, Srok Dong and Minh Thanh Road (June-July), then Operation Attleboro in November. In February 1967, the Division participated in Operations Cedar Falls, Junction City, Manhattan and Shenandoah II. On 17 October, the Big Red One was engaged in the battle of Ong Thanh, where it suffered heavy losses (58 killed). It played a part in repulsing the Tet Offensive in 1968 and held the Tan Son Nhut hills near the air base. In March, the Division took part in Operation Resolve to Win and in April, it deployed its troops in the biggest operation of the entire war, called 'Toan Thang' (Complete victory). On 13 September, the divisional commander, Major General Ware, was killed when his helicopter was shot down by enemy fire. During the first half of 1969, the Big Red One carried out a war of patrols and ambushes, as well as taking part in Operation Atlas Wedge. Throughout the second half, it supported South-Vietnamese forces which were taking on an increasingly active role. In August, the Division fought along National Route 13. In January 1970, the 1st Division returned to Fort Riley. Eleven of its men had won the Medal of Honor. The Division lost 6,146 men killed in action and 16,019 wounded in Vietnam.

Below.
A C Company, 26th Infantry squad during a sweep in the Al Adhamiya region near Baghdad, 27 March 2007.
(US Army)

Below.
A GI from Company C, 26th Infantry, keeps an eye on the slopes of a valley during a patrol in Afghanistan, 6 April 2009.
(US Army)

Desert Storm

The 1st Division took part in 'Desert Storm' in 1991. During the start of the allied ground offensive on 24 February, it opened a gap in the enemy lines along the Iraq-Saudi Arabia border. The 26th Iraqi division was destroyed and 2,600 prisoners taken. In the space of four days, the Big Red One advanced 260 km into enemy territory, engaging eleven divisions, destroying 550 tanks and 480 armored vehicles and taking a total of 11,400 prisoners. On 28 February, the Big Red One took up positions along 'Death Highway,' preventing any retreat undertaken by Iraqi forces from Kuwait. The next month, after the capitulation, it returned to the United States.

In 1996, the Division was moved to Würzburg, Germany. The 2nd Brigade was deployed to Bosnia in order to take part in peacekeeping operations until April 1997. From August 1999 to April 2000, elements of the 1st Brigade were once more deployed to Bosnia and other units of the Division served in Kosovo up to 2003. Since 2006, still stationed at Fort Riley, Kansas, the division has taken part in the Global war on terrorism in Iraq and Afghanistan.

12 - The Big Red One in facts and figures

WW2 CAMPAIGNS

Algeria-French Morocco
Tunisia
Sicily
Normandy
Northern France
Rhineland
Ardennes-Alsace
Central Europe

For each campaign, a soldier was authorized to wear a star on the European-African-Middle Eastern Campaign medal ribbon, with the exception of landings (Algeria, Sicily; Normandy), symbolized by an arrowhead.

1st INFANTRY DIVISION ESTIMATED TOTAL CASUALTIES

Killed in action	3,616
Wounded in action	15,208
Died of wounds	664

OVERSEAS ASSIGNMENTS

- North African Theater of Operations, 8 November 1942
- II Corps, 1 February 1943
- 1st Army, 1 November 1943
- VII Corps, 6 November 1943
- V Corps, 2 February 1944
- 1st Army, 14 July 1944
- VII Corps, 1 August 1944
- V Corps, 16 December 1944
- XVIII (A/B) Corps, 26 January 1945
- III Corps, 12 February 1945
- VII Corps, 8 March 1945
- VIII Corps, 27 April 1945
- V Corps, 30 April 1945
- 3rd Army, 6 May 1945
- XV Corps, 30 June 1945

DIVISIONAL COMMAND STRUCTURE

● Commanding general:
Major General Donald Cubbison: July 1941
Major General Terry de la Mesa Allen: July 1942
Major General Clarence R. Huebner: July 1943
Major General Clift Andrus: December 1944

● Assistant division commander:
Brigadier General Willard G. Wyman, November 1943
Brigadier General George A. Taylor, October 1944

● Divisional Artillery:
Brigadier General Clift Andrus 5 Nov. 1943
Colonel William E. Waters, 14 December 1944
Brigadier General William E. Waters, March 1945

● Chief of Staff:
Colonel Norman D. Cota, August 1942
Colonel Stanhope B. Mason, November 1943
Lt. Colonel Clarence E. Beck, December 1944
Colonel Verdi B. Barnes, 7 January 1945

● Assistant Chief of Staff G-1 (personnel)
Lt. Colonel Charles S. Ware, November 1943

● Assistant Chief of Staff G-2 (intelligence)
Maj. Robert F. Evans, 5 November 1943
Lt. Colonel Verdi B. Barnes, 9 November 1943
Major Robert F. Evans, 27 November 1943
Lt. Colonel Robert F. Evans, April 1944
Maj. John H. Lauten, 9 April 1945

● Assistant Chief of Staff G-3 (training and operations)
Lt. Colonel Frederick W. Gibb, November 1943
Lt. Colonel Clarence E. Beck, July 1944
Major Kenneth B. Lord, 14 December 1944
Lt. Colonel Clarence E. Beck, 7 Jan. 1945

● Assistant Chief of Staff G-4 (supply)
Lt. Colonel Verdi B. Barnes, 5 November 1943
Lt. Colonel Clarence M. Eymer, 19 November 1943
Lt. Colonel Donald M. Curtis, 14 December 1944

● Assistant Chief of Staff G-5 (civil affairs)
Lt. Colonel John M. Rogers, Jr., 5 November 1943
Major Thomas F. Lancer, 15 August 1944
Lt. Colonel Thomas F. Lancer, 5 November 1944

● Adjutant General (administration)
Lt. Colonel Leonidas Gavalas, 5 November 1943
Maj. Leander A. Dailey, 11 February 1945

● Commanding Officer, 16th Infantry
Colonel Henry B. Cheadle
Colonel George A. Taylor, 5 November 1943
Colonel Frederick W. Gibb, 15 July 1944

● Commanding Officer, 18th Infantry
Colonel Frank U. Greer
Colonel George Smith, Jr., 5 November 1943
Colonel John Williamson, 25 February 1945

● Commanding Officer, 26th Infantry
Colonel Alexander N. Stark Jr.
Colonel John W. Bowen, 5 November 1943
Colonel John F. R. Seitz, 14 November 1943
Colonel Francis J. Murdoch, Jr., 9 April 1945

1st DIVISION AWARDS

The personnel of the following units were allowed to wear the blue and gold badge of the Distinguished Unit Citation: 16th Infantry, 18th Infantry, 1/26th Infantry, 32nd FA Bn, 1st Eng. Bn, 1st Signal Co.

Foreign Awards :
- All division personnel were allowed to wear the French fourragere in the green and red colours of the Croix de Guerre, for Kasserine and the Normandy Landings
- the division was also awarded the Belgian fourragère (red and green) for its compaigns of September (liberation) and December 1944 (the Bulge) in this country.

INDIVIDUAL AWARDS

Medal of Honor (read following pages)	16
Distinguished Service Cross	131
Legion of Merit	16
Silver Star	4,258
Soldier's Medal	100
Bronze Star	12,568
Air Medal	65

The route of the 1st Infantry Division from England to Czechoslovakia

Location of divisional command post: date, town, region, country

1942

7 August Glasgow Lanarkshire Scotland
9 August Tidworth Barracks Wiltshire England
22 October Leaves for North Africa

1943

7 November Liverpool Lancashire
9 November Blandford Dorset England

1944

3 June Portland Dorset England
6 June Omaha Beach Calvados France
7 June Colleville-sur-Mer Calvados France
8 June Russy Calvados France
10 June Court Elay Calvados France
11 June Sur-Le-Chemin-du-Gril Calvados France
12 June Balleroy Calvados France
14 July Colombières Calvados France
20 July Saint-Jean-de-Daye Manche France
25 July Bois du Hommat Manche France
28 July La Chapelle Manche France
28 July Marigny Manche France
30 July Saint-Denis-du-Gast Manche France
1 August Brecey Manche France
3 August Juvigny Manche France
4 August Logis du Bocage Manche France
7 August Logis du Bocage Manche France
13 August Ambrières le Grand Mayenne France
13 August La Ferté-Macé Orne France
14 August Couterne Orne France
15 August Bagnoles de l'Orne Orne France
24 August Le Thieulin Eure-et-Loir France
25 August Lardy Seine-et-Oise France
27 August Etiolles Seine-et-Oise France
27 August Servon Seine-et-Marne France
28 August Maison Rothschild (Ferrières) Seine-et-Marne France
28 August Quincy-Voisins Seine-et-Oise France
29 August Crouy Seine-et-Marne France
30 August Soissons Aisne France
31 August Chevrigny Aisne France
1 Sept. Missy Aisne France
2 Sept. Le Novion Aisne France
3 Sept. Ecuelin Nord France
4 Sept. Mons Hainault Belgium
6 Sept. Roux Hainault Belgium
7 Sept. Namur Belgium
8 Sept. Stockay Namur Belgium
11 Sept. Lalouxe Namur Belgium
14 Sept. Henri-Chapelle Liège Belgium
15 Sept. Hauset (7 km Aix la ch.) Liège Belgium
10 November Vicht Rhineland Germany
8 December Hauset Liège Belgium
17 December Sourbrodt Liège Belgium

1945

27 Jan. Weverce Liège Belgium
1 February Hunningen Liège Belgium
6 February Aywaille Liège Belgium
8 February Grosshau Rhineland Germany
28 February Drove Rhineland Germany
2 March Kelz Rhineland Germany
6 March Friesham Rhineland Germany
7 March Metternich Rhineland Germany
15 March Unkel Rhineland Germany
21 March Ittenbach Rhineland Germany
24 March Oberpleis Rhineland Germany
27 March Obereip Rhineland Germany
28 March Eichelhardt Rhineland Germany
29 March Allendorf Nassau Germany
31 March Biedenkopf Nassau Germany
1 April Wunnenberg Westphalia Germany
7 April Peckelsheim Westphalia Germany
9 April Lauenforde Hannover Germany
10 April Uslar Hannover Germany
11 April Northeim Hannover Germany
12 April Osterode Hannover Germany
17 April St Andreasberg Hannover Germany
19 April Benneckenstein Brunswick Germany
24 April Blankenheim Halle-Merseburg Germany
27 April Markleuthen Bavaria Germany
6 May Cheb Sudeten Czechoslovakia

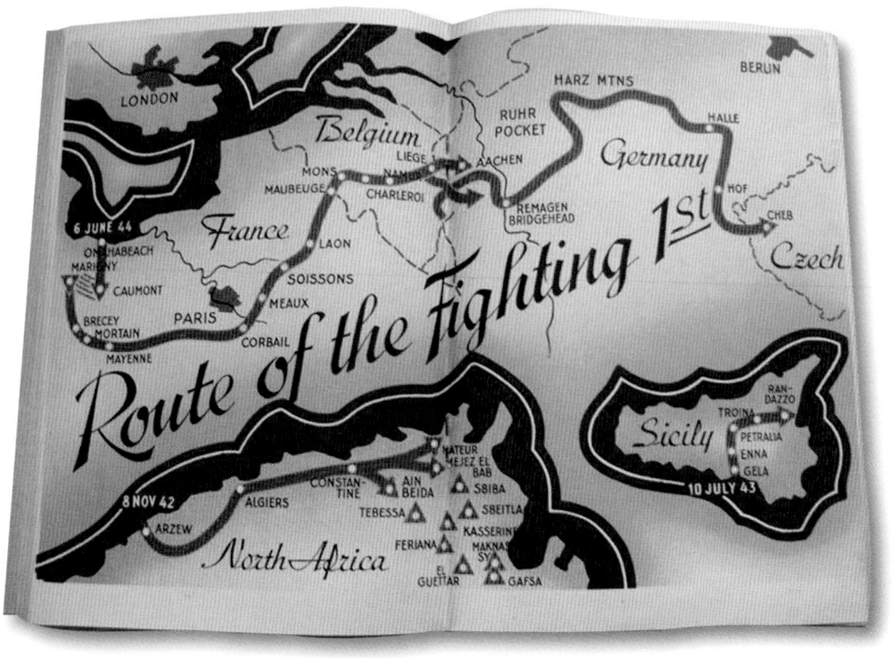

"The First," a booklet telling of the odyssey of the Division throughout the Second World War. (Michel Pascal collection)

The Big Red One shoulder patch

The 1st Division shoulder patch was officially approved by the American Expeditionary Force (AEF) headquarters on 31 October 1918 and comprised of a red number 1.

According to the legend, the first patches, a straightforward number 1 cut from red cloth, were cut from the red band of German field caps (Feldmütze).

This booklet was printed in Paris at the end of the war and given to every soldier in the Division prior to returning home.
(Michel Pascal collection)

- 1. 1930-1940 period, light khaki twill for the summer uniform
- 2 & 3. Same period, embroidered on olive drab wool for the winter uniform.
- 4. Standard manufacture, WW2, fully embroidered.
- 5. Variation, darker background.
- 6. Variation, very light background.
- 7. Theater-made in North Africa or Sicily 1943. The number is roughly cut out and sewn on a herringbone twill background.
- 8. British-made patch, 1943-45.
- 9. European-made, 1944-1945, number embroidered in red and highlighted with gold bullion, gilt cord around the border.
- 10. Woven European-made patch, possibly German.

(Pierre Besnard Collection, extract from Militaria Guide No 6, US Army insignia 1941-1945, vol. I, Histoire & Collections 2013)

Units attached to the 1st Infantry Division

ANTIAIRCRAFT ARTILLERY

Btry B, 103d AAA AW Bn 12-15 June 1944
Btry D, 461st AAA AW Bn 15-28 June 1944
103d AAA AW Bn 16 June 1944-7 Feb. 1945
Btrys B & D, 461st AAA AW
Bn 26-28 June 1944
Btrys A&D, 486th AAA AW Bn
(SP) 6-30 July 1944
Btry B, 413th AAA Gun Bn
(Mbl) 6-30 July 1944
Btry A, 413th AAA Gun Bn (Mbl)
31 July -11 August 1944
Btrys A&D, 486th AAA AW Bn
(SP) 5-6 August 1944
Btry B, 413th AAA Gun Bn
(Mbl) 5-6 August 1944
639th AAA AW Bn 18-31 December 1944
Btry A, 460th AAA AW Bn 1 Jan. 1945
103d AAA AW Bn (Mbl) 24 Feb.-8 May 1945

ARMORED FORCE

(tank battalions, armored infantry, engineers and artillery)

745th Tank Bn 6 June 1944-8 May 1945
747th Tank Bn 7-13 June 1944
741st Tank Bn 7-15 June 1944
743d Tank Bn 11-13 June 1944
3d Armd Gp (- 747th Tk Bn) 11-15 June 1944
CCB/3d Armd Div. 6-30 July 1944
33d Armd Regt (3d Armd Div) 6-30 July 1944
36th Armd Inf (-3d Bn) (3d
Armd Div) 6-30 July 1944
391st Armd FA Bn (3d Armd
Div) 6-30 July 1944
83d Armd Rcn Bn (3d Armd
Div) 6-30 July 1944
Cos B&D, 23d Armd Engr Bn (3d
Armd Div) 6-30 July 1944
87th Armd FA Bn 6-30 July 1944
CCA/3d Armd Div 31 July -11 August 1944
32d Armd Regt (3d Armd Div)
31 July -11 August 1944
3d Bn, 36th Armd Inf (3d Armd
Div) 31 July -11 August 1944
54th Armd FA Bn (3d Armd Div)
31 juil-11 August 1944
67th Armd FA Bn (3d Armd Div)
31 July -11 August 1944
Cos A&C, 23d Armd Engr Bn (3d Armd
Div) 31 July -11 August 1944
58th Armd FA Bn 31 July -11 August 1944
CCB/3d Armd Div 5-6 August 1944
33d Armd Regt (3d Armd
Div) 5-6 August 1944
36th Armd Inf (-3d Bn) (3d Armd
Div) 5-6 August 1944
391st Armd FA Bn (3d Armd
Div) 5-6 August 1944
83d Armd Rcn Bn (3d Armd
Div) 5-6 August 1944
Cos B&D, 23d Armd Engr Bn (3d
Armd Div) 5-6 August 1944
87th Armd FA Bn 5-6 August 1944
CCR/3d Armd Div 8-17 March 1945
3d Bn, 32d Armd Regt (3d Armd
Div) 8-17 March 1945
2d Bn, 33d Armd Regt (3d Armd
Div) 8-17 March 1945
3d Bn, 36th Armd Inf (3d Armd
Div) 8-17 March 1945
Co C, 23d Armd Engr Bn (3d
Armd Div) 8-17 March 1945
3d Bn, 13th Inf (8th Div) 8-17 March 1945
CCR/3d Armd Div. 20-21 March 1945
3d Bn, 32d Armd Regt (3d Armd
Div) 20-21 March 1945
2d Bn, 33d Armd Regt (3d Armd
Div) 20-21 March 1945
3d Bn, 36th Armd Inf (3d Armd
Div) 20-21 March 1945
Co C, 23d Armd Engr Bn (3d Armd
Div) 20-21 March 1945
3d Bn, 13th Inf (8th Div) 20-21 March 1945
CCA/9th Armd Div. 4-8 May 1945

CAVALRY

102d Cav Rcn Sq 11-13 June 1944

TANK DESTROYERS

(self-propelled)
634th TD Battalion, 1 August
1944-6 May 1945
635th TD Battalion,
7 June-30 September 1944
Cos B&C (-3d Plat.), 703d
TD Bn 6-30 July 1944
Co A & 3d Plat./Co B, 703d TD Bn
(SP) 31 July -11 August 1944
Cos B&C (-3d Plat.), 703d TD
Bn 5-6 August 1944
703rd TD Battalion, 18-31 December 1944
Co C, 703d TD Bn 8-17 March 1945
Co C, 703d TD Bn 20-21 March 1945

Key to abbreviations:
AW: auto(matic) weapons
CCA: Combat Command A
CCB: Combat Command B
CCR: Combat Command Reserve
FA : Field Artillery
Gp: Group
Mbl: Mobile
Rcn: Reconnaissance

Distinctive unit insignia worn on garrison caps and lapels (enlisted) and shoulder straps (officers) of the service coat.
1. 16th Infantry Regiment
2. 18th Infantry Regiment
3. 26th Infantry Regiment
4. 5th Field Artillery Battalion
5. 7th Field Artillery Battalion
6. 32nd Field Artillery Battalion
7. 33rd Field Artillery Battalion
8. 1st Engineer Combat Battalion
9. 1st Medical Battalion
10. 1st Signal Company
11. 1st Cavalry reconnaissance Troop, Mechanized.
12. 745th Tank Battalion.
(Yves Le Clair collection)

13 - Big Red One Division senior officers and heroes

THE EHLERS BROTHERS' STORY

Roland A. Ehlers was born on 28 November 1917, and his younger brother, Walter David 'Walt' on 21 May 1921, at Junction City (Kansas). The two brothers joined up in October 1940 and served in a rifle company, with the 7th, then 3rd Division. Their training continued until the beginning of October 1942, the date on which they left, with their division, for North Africa. They were then transferred to the 18th Infantry and landed in Sicily. During the fighting, Roland was wounded by mortar shell splinters and half buried by the explosion. He was evacuated to Africa for treatment. In November 1943, the Division was sent to England in order to prepare for D-Day. Roland was reunited with Walt in Company K. In March 1944 they were split up due to administrative reasons and Walt was promoted to staff sergeant in Company L. Just prior to D-Day, Roland and Walt saw each other in Weymouth whilst waiting to board their LCI. They said farewell to each other and promised to meet up on the beach. They were both part of the second wave on Omaha Beach. LCI 487, in which Roland Ehlers was placed, was hit by an 88 shell at the moment the ramps were lowered. Shortly after landing, during a brief respite, Walt went off to look for Roland. He did not receive any news of his brother until 14 July when he learned that he had been killed on 6 June before he even set foot on the beach. On 9 June, Walt showed great courage in the fighting at Goville and was awarded the Medal of Honor. Walter D. Ehlers survived the war and died on 20 February 2014 at the age of 92.

The Ehlers brothers in 1940, Roland (left), and Walt during their basic training at Fort Ord, California (also read the Medal of Honor chapter)

Staff Sergeant Walter D. Ehlers seen here in 1945.

TERRY DE LA MESA ALLEN (1888-1969)

Terry Allen was born on 1 April 1888 at Fort Douglas, Utah. He was the son of Colonel Samuel Allen and part of a long line of professional soldiers. His maternal grandfather was colonel Carlos Alvarez de la Mesa, a Spaniard who had fought with the Union army at Gettysburg. Allen grew up in various camps according to where his father was posted. He spent time with enlisted men, sharing their hobbies, their way of speaking and their habits. In 1907, he was recommended for West Point. He soon failed, however, due to a lack of discipline and missing theory lessons. After studying at the Catholic University of Washington and a telling off from his father, he passed an officers' school exam and became a second lieutenant. He was posted to the 14th Cavalry in Texas in 1913, and chased bandits and smugglers along the Mexican border. Promoted to lieutenant on 1 July 1916, he rose to the rank of captain on 15 May 1917. On 7 June 1918, Allen was sent to France and attached to an artillery supply train, then to the 358th Infantry, 90th Division. During the course of a battle, he was hit in the jaw by a bullet. He ended the war with a Silver Star for bravery. He would stop at nothing to spare his men's lives and on more than one occasion suffered lower losses by ordering a coordinated daytime attack to be undertaken at night. Allen remained with the army of occupation in Germany until 1920. Upon his return to the United States, he was promoted to major and joined the 61st Cavalry Division in New York in 1922, then the famous 7th Cavalry at Fort Riley (Kansas). On 1 August 1935, Allen was promoted to lieutenant-colonel and became an instructor at the Fort Riley cavalry school. He wrote a manual, in 1939, entitled *Reconnaissance by horse cavalry regiments and smaller units*. On 1 October 1940, he was promoted by General Marshall to the rank of brigadier general and, in 1942, rose to the rank of major general, taking command of the 1st Division in Florida. Marshall, Chief of Staff of the Army, had noticed Allen at the Infantry School, and said: *"Allen might not have a long peacetime career, but if we go to war, we will have to give him a division"*. As soon as he took over command of the 1st Division, he stood out by his charisma and leadership skills, winning the respect and loyalty of his men. However, Allen was no stickler for discipline and regulations as he considered that respect and obedience could only be obtained by esprit de corps and a closeness between officers and enlisted men. He stated that *"a soldier does not fight to save oppressed people or nonsense like that. He fights to prove that his outfit is the best in the entire Army and that he has as much guts as his buddies"*.

Major General Terry Allen in Sicily, 1943.

In North Africa, with the British and American allies fighting alongside each other for the first

Brigadier General Theodore Roosevelt Jr. in North Africa.

time, the Division found itself up against a very tough adversary and paled due to a lack of co-ordination at senior officer level. Always at the sharp end, Allen was already worn out at the end of the Tunisian campaign. In July 1943 and barely over licking its wounds, the Division took part in the Sicily landings upon the insistence of Patton. Both cavalrymen, Patton and Allen were fairly close, despite the fact that the former kept up a provocative rivalry with his friend. During a visit to the divisional HQ, at that time the target of regular Luftwaffe raids, Patton asked where Allen's slit trench was and then proceeded to urinate in it... At the end of this campaign, Terry Allen was relieved by Bradley who did not like his subordinate's independent spirit and the Big Red One's superiority complex. On 7 August 1943, Allen was replaced by General Clarence Huebner. Terry Allen was sent home, officially for a rest period but, in October 1943, was given the command of the 104th Infantry Division, the Timberwolves, whose training he completed in his own way and which he led brilliantly into combat. This division landed in France on 7 September 1944, Belgium on 21 October, Holland on the 30th, and into Germany on 7 November 1944. In June 1946, the 104th Infantry Division was deactivated upon its return to the United States. A disillusioned Terry Allen left the Army and retired to Texas on 31 August the same year. For a few years he worked as an insurance salesman, then in civil affairs and for veterans associations. His own son, Lieutenant-Colonel Terry de la Mesa Allen Jr. was killed in action in Vietnam in October 1967 whilst commanding the 2nd Battalion, 28th Infantry.

Terry de la Mesa Allen died aged 81 on 12 September 1969 at El Paso in Texas. He lies at rest with his wife and son at the Fort Bliss cemetery. Today, the West Point Academy awards a "General Terry de la Mesa Allen" prize in military science. It is ironic, given that Allen had failed at West Point and that he often complained throughout his career of having been overlooked for promotion because he was not a member of the WPPA ('West Point Protective Association')...

THEODORE ROOSEVELT JUNIOR (1887-1944)

Teddy Roosevelt Junior was born in 1887 on Long Island, at a time when his father (president of the United States from 1901 to 1909 and cousin of Franklin Roosevelt, president from 1933 to 1945) was taking his first steps in politics. Having studied at Harvard, he went into business and was successful in steel mills, then the banking sector. Throughout his life, he strove to be equal to his father, a fearless soldier and one of the most popular presidents. Following military training, he was amongst the first to volunteer for American Expeditionary Force in France in 1917. His qualities were noticed and he was given command of the 26th Infantry, 1st Division. He was wounded and gassed at Château-Thierry in July 1918. For his service in France, he was awarded the DSC, Silver Star, Croix de guerre and Légion d'honneur. Upon his return to the United States he began a political career and occupied several public positions. A colonel in 1940, he was once again given command of the 26th Infantry. Promoted to general at the end of 1941, he became second in command of the Big Red One in August 1942. He participated in the fighting in North Africa and was well-liked by his men due to his frequent visits to the front-line, preferring action to the comfort of the HQ. His commanding officer, Terry Allen, shared the same outlook. The same could not be said of General Bradley who did not like the two men and who eventually sacked them. Although they were excellent leaders, they were deemed as being too close to their men and tolerating certain forms of indiscipline. Also, Roosevelt did not have the dash of other generals. According to his aide-de-camp *"Most of the time he forgot to put on his helmet, which in any case he did not know how to wear properly, and when wearing his combat uniform, he was the scruffiest GI there was."*

It is worth mentioning that during the debacle at Kasserine, Roosevelt almost lost his son Quentin. The latter was an artillery officer and was hit in the lungs by a bullet during a strafe by Luftwaffe planes. He barely survived. After a period as a liaison officer with the Canadians in Italy, he was finally sent to England and the 4th Infantry Division as second in command to General Barton. The high command was loath to risk a Roosevelt being killed on the Normandy beaches, but in a long letter to Barton, Theodore Junior pleaded to be allowed to take part. The 4th Division commander, no doubt himself under political pressure, accepted as Roosevelt was popular with the men and his presence would be an asset in the first uncertain minutes of the assault. Weakened by a bout of pneumonia, Roosevelt landed at the head of his men with the help of a walking stick on 6 June at Utah Beach. The landing craft had drifted a great deal and the first wave found itself a kilometer away from the designated area. After having set foot on land, Roosevelt said to his men, "Never mind, we'll start the war from here!" However, on 12 July 1944 at Méautis, after a long and tough day of German counter-attacks, "Teddy" Roosevelt passed away from a heart attack during the night. Shortly before his death, General Barton had recommended him for the Distinguished Service Cross, but Roosevelt was actually posthumously awarded the Medal of Honor. Theodore Roosevelt Jr. lies at rest with his men in the last row of section D at the American cemetery of Colleville sur-Mer. He was portrayed by the actor Henry Fonda in the movie, *The Longest Day*.

Major General Clarence Huebner seen here in Germany, 1944. In this color photograph, the divisional patch is clearly visible on the steel helmet.

CLARENCE RALPH HUEBNER (1888-1972)

Clarence Huebner was born on 24 November 1888, in Bushton (Kansas). He worked as a farm hand before enlisting in 1910. As an NCO with the 18th Infantry, he took part in the Mexican border operations in 1916. A soldier of great aptitude, he was put forward for officers' school the same year. During the First World War, Lieutenant Huebner served with the 2/28th Infantry, 1st Division and saw action at Cantigny, Soissons, Saint-Mihiel and in the Meuse-Argonne offensive. He received a head wound whilst patrolling near Toul in March 1918; a bullet pierced the rim of his helmet and hit him between the eyes! At the end of the war he was in command of the 18th Infantry with the temporary rank of lieutenant-colonel. During the course of his service in France he was awarded two Distinguished Service Crosses, two Purple Hearts, a Silver Star, plus the Légion d'honneur and the Croix de guerre. Upon his return to the United States he was posted, for the first time, as instructor at the new Infantry School of Fort Benning.

Brigadier General Clift Andrus commanded the divisional artillery and replaced Huebner in December 1944.

He went to the Command and General Staff School at Fort Leavenworth in 1924, where future senior officers were groomed, returning there as an instructor from 1929 to 1933. Promoted to Major in 1927, Huebner continued his rise by passing out of the Army War College, a must for aspiring generals. In the meantime, he was assigned once more to the Infantry School as a cs instructor and was noticed by the school commandant, George Marshall, who added him to the list of promising officers whose careers he would follow. Then, in 1934, he was posted to the office of the Chief of Infantry in Washington. Promoted to lieutenant-colonel in 1938, Huebner spent the next four years between Hawaii, Washington and various postings in the United States. At GHQ from 1940 to 1942, he supervised the creation and training of large units. In July 1943, he replaced Terry Allen as commander of the 1st Division and led it with a firm and skilled hand from Normandy to Germany. In January 1945, Huebner took command of V Corps, leading it from the Rhineland to the Elbe, where his troops were the first to link up with the Red Army. He was replaced as commanding officer of the Big Red One by General Andrus. After the Second World War, Huebner became the last military governor (temporary) of the American zone in Germany from 15 May to 1 September 1949. After retiring in 1950, he led the Civil Defence for the State of New York. Clarence Ralph Huebner died on 23 September 1972 in Washington, he lies at rest in Arlington National Cemetery.

CLIFT ANDRUS (1890-1968)

Clift Andrus, son of Colonel Edwin Proctor Andrus, was born on 12 October 1890 at Fort Leavenworth, Kansas. He joined the Army in 1912 as a second lieutenant with the 4th Artillery. In 1914 and 1915, he was posted to the Mexican border following the violent incursions by Pancho Villa. Throughout the First World War, Andrus was an instructor at the Artillery School in Fort Sill. At the beginning of the Second World War, Colonel Andrus was in command of the 24th Division artillery garrisoned at Schofield Barracks (Hawaii). He became a brigadier general in May 1942 in order to take command of the 1st Division's artillery. In North Africa, he was awarded, amongst others, with the Distinguished Service Cross and Silver Star. Andrus replaced General Huebner in December 1944 and commanded the Division until the end of the war. From 1946 to 1949, Clift Andrus commanded the Artillery School in Oklahoma, before being assigned to the general staff at Washington where he became head of organization and training. His final posting was as second in command of the 2nd Army at Fort Meade (Maryland), after which he retired in October 1952. Clift Andrus died in Washington on 29 September 1958 and was buried at the Arlington National Cemetery.

Brigadier General Wyman was second in command of the Big Red One from November 1943 to October 1944. He distinguished himself at Omaha Beach in pursuing the attack beyond the beach.

WILLARD GORDON WYMAN (1898-1969)

Willard G. Wyman was born on 21 March 1898 in Augusta, Maine. In 1919, he passed out of West Point. During the Second World War he served with the 9th Corps headquarters, then in 1942 with that of the China-Burma-India Theater of Operations. Attached to General Joseph Stilwell's staff, he took part in the long retreat on foot from Burma. From 1942 to 1943, he served at Allied Forces HQ in North Africa before being assigned as second in command of the 1st Division in November 1943. On 6 June, Wyman landed on Omaha Beach shortly after 8 in the morning. He was awarded the Distinguished Service Cross for his vital role in the attack beyond the beach and the reorganization of units pinned down on the shingle. In October 1944, General Wyman took command of the 71st Infantry Division. During the Korean War, he commanded IX Army Corps before being named as commander in chief of NATO forces from 1952 to 1954. He then went on to serve as commander of 6th Army from 1954 to 1955. His last position was that of chief of the Continental Army Command (CONARC). He retired from the Army in 1958. Willard Gordon Wyman died on 29 March 1969 in Washington DC, he lies at rest in the Arlington National Cemetery. He was awarded the following decorations throughout his career: the Distinguished Service Cross, Distinguished Service Medal with three Oak Leaves, Silver Star, Legion of Merit and Bronze Star.

GEORGE ARTHUR TAYLOR (1899-1969)

George A. Taylor was born on 14 February 1899 at Flat Rock (Illinois). He graduated from West Point with the class of 1922. Up to 1930, Taylor occupied various positions in the infantry. In 1937, he was posted to the Philippines Scouts. Upon his return home, he was assigned to the 16th Infantry where he was promoted to intelligence officer for the 1st Battalion. In 1941, he was a tactics instructor at the Fort Benning Infantry School. When the United States entered the war, he was transferred to North Africa as liaison officer with the amphibious forces of the Atlantic Fleet. February 1943 saw his brief transfer to the 26th Infantry before joining, on 20 April, the 16th Infantry as commanding officer, leading his men into action in Sicily. At 8 o'clock on 6 June, he arrived with the second wave on Omaha Beach. He found the survivors of the first wave pinned down, shocked and exhausted. It was then that he shouted his famous words: "There are two kinds of people who are staying on this beach: those who are dead and those who are going to die. Now let's get the hell out of here!"

Here is his citation for the award of the Distinguished Service Cross, 14 June 1944: "Col. George A. Taylor, in command of the 16th RCT, landed during the most crucial, threatening period of the operation. Thousands of leaderless men lay huddled on the seven-yard beachhead, their organization disastrously cut down by fire. The exists were blocked, supporting weapons had not or could not be landed or were already destroyed, and the attack was arrested. Without hesitation, unmindful of the snipers and machine gun fire directed at him, Taylor moved up and down the beach, continuously exposing himself to murderous fire. He found officers and gathered groups of men together for them to lead. He found, led, and drove men into the action. Calmly and coolly he assigned objectives to these newly organized groups. He converted a bewildered mob into a coordinated fighting force."

Taylor was promoted to brigadier general on 1 August 1944 and became second in command of the 1st Division from October 1944 to July 1945. He retired in 1946 because of health issues. After a long illness, he died on 3 December 1969 at Palo Alto, California. In the movie, *The Longest Day*, the script writers linked his character to that of General Cota, played by Robert Mitchum, erroneously giving the latter the famous words shouted out on Omaha Beach. Both officers had played a similar role, separated by a few hundred meters on the same beach.

Colonel George Taylor, commander of the 16th Infantry, was awarded the Distinguished Service Cross for his actions at dawn 6 June on Omaha Beach.

1st Infantry Division Medal of Honor recipients

CARLTON WILLIAM BARRETT (1919-1986)

Carlton W. Barrett hailed from Fulton, in the State of New York. He enlisted in the 18th Infantry in October 1940 and received the Medal of Honor for his actions on D-Day. His citation reads as follows: "Citation: For gallantry and intrepidity at the risk of his life above and beyond the call of duty on 6 June, in the vicinity of St. Laurent-sur-Mer, France. On the morning of D-day Pvt. Barrett, landing in the face of extremely heavy enemy fire, was forced to wade ashore through neck-deep water. Disregarding the personal danger, he returned to the surf again and again to assist his floundering comrades and save them from drowning. Refusing to remain pinned down by the intense barrage of small-arms and mortar fire poured at the landing points, Pvt. Barrett, working with fierce determination, saved many lives by carrying casualties to an evacuation boat Lying offshore. In addition to his assigned mission as guide, he carried dispatches the length of the fire-swept beach; he assisted the wounded; he calmed the shocked; he arose as a leader in the stress of the occasion. His coolness and his dauntless daring courage while constantly risking his life during a period of many hours had an inestimable effect on his comrades and is in keeping with the highest traditions of the U.S. Army."

Right, Carlton Barrett.

Barrett was one of three men to receive the highest American decoration during D-Day, all of whom were from the Big Red One. He continued to serve in the Army until his retirement on June 1963 with the rank of staff sergeant. Carlton W. Barrett died on 3 May 1986 and was buried at Napa, California.

Lieutenant Walter J. Will

Sergeant Max Thompson

MAX THOMPSON (1922-1996)

Max Thompson was born on 21 July 1922 at Bethel, North Carolina. He worked in a paper mill before enlisting on 14 November 1942. He was inducted at Camp Croft, South Carolina with Company K, 18th Infantry. During the course of the fighting north-east of Aachen in October 1944, Sergeant Thompson was evacuating wounded men of another platoon who had been heavily engaged by a counter-attack. Then, by using any weapon available (a machine-gun, bazooka and BAR light machine-gun) he managed to halt the attack. He was awarded the Medal of Honor the following summer. Thompson died at the age of 74 on 30 November 1996 and lies at rest at Forest Lawn cemetery, Candler, North Carolina.

WALTER J. WILL (1922-1945)

Walter Will enlisted in December 1940. On 30 March 1945, he was a lieutenant with Company K, 18th Infantry. During the course of a fire-fight near Eisern, Germany, he saved three of his men who had just been wounded. He was himself hit in the hand, but managed to knock out two machine-gun nests and lead his platoon on to the capture of two other positions. However, he was mortally wounded whilst leading a charge against the enemy. Lieutenant Will was posthumously awarded the Medal of Honor seven months later on 17 October 1945. He was buried at the American Cemetery at Margraten, Holland.

Henry F. Warner.

HENRY F. WARNER (1921-1944)

Henry F. Warner, from North Carolina, was drafted in January 1943. On 20 December 1944 in the Ardennes, he was a corporal with the anti-tank platoon of the 2nd Bn./26th Infantry. He was in position at Bütgenbach with his 57mm gun and under intense artillery fire when faced with a panzer attack with infantry support. He knocked out several tanks before being mortally wounded. Warner was posthumously awarded the Medal of Honor on 23 June 1945. He lies in the Southside cemetery in North Carolina.

BOBBIE E. BROWN (1903-1971)

Robert "Bobbie" Evan Brown Jr. was born in Dublin, Georgia in 1903. In 1922 he lied about his age in order to enlist. When the Second World War broke out, he was first sergeant with the headquarters company of the 2nd Armored Division commanded by General Patton. After having fought in North Africa, he was promoted to lieutenant and transferred to the 1st Infantry Division. He commanded a platoon of Company C, 18th Infantry up to Omaha Beach on 6 june 1944. On that day he replaced his company commander who had been killed in action. At Aachen on 8 October 1944, he took part in the attack on Crucifix Hill, an area strongly defended by 43 bunkers. Following an air strike by P-47 Thunderbolts, he rushed forward with his men and single-handedly knocked out several positions, including a bunker housing an 88mm gun. He escaped with a slight knee wound.

Far right, Lieutenant Walter Ehlers in December 1944 in Paris, where he was awarded the Medal of Honor.

During the course of street fighting in the town, he was once more wounded by shell fragments. After several months in a Belgian hospital, he returned home for 30 days furlough before returning to his company in Germany. He was awarded the Medal of Honor on 23 August 1945 for his actions at Aachen. Despite the 13 wounds received during the war, he ended his 30 years of service in 1952. As well as the Medal of Honor, Brown won two Silver Stars, a Bronze Star and the Purple Heart.

Suffering from post-traumatic stress, he was unable to find stable employment in civilian life and became a janitor at the West Point Military Academy. On 8 November 1971, haunted by his combat experiences and wracked with pain from his wounds, he committed suicide by shooting himself in the chest. He lies at rest in the Arlington National Cemetery near the tomb of the Unknown Soldiers.

Bobbie E. Brown.

THE MEDAL OF HONOR

The medal was established on 12 December 1861; the fourth type for the Army (1944) is seen here. It is the highest American military honor and is awarded for personal acts of valor, above and beyond the call of duty.

WALTER DAVID EHLERS (1921-2014)

Walter D. Ehlers enlisted in 1940 in Kansas at the same time as his brother Roland (see page 87). On 6 June, Walter Ehlers was a squad leader with the 18th Infantry, his assault team was part of the second wave. On 9 June, near Goville, a village 13 kilometers inland, he single-handedly knocked out several machine-guns.

The next day, his platoon was pinned down by heavy fire. Ehlers was wounded, but managed to cover his men's withdrawal. After being

Arthur DeFranzo.

bandaged up, the NCO refused to be evacuated and continued leading his squad. He was awarded the Medal of Honor for these actions on 19 December 1944.

Walter D. Ehlers played in the movie *The Long Gray Line* directed by John Ford, in 1955, with Tyrone Power. He went on to work for the Veterans Administration and as a security guard at Disneyland, in California. Walter D. Ehlers died on 20 February 2014, he lies at rest at the Riverside National Cemetery in California. His Medal of Honor is on display at the National WW2 Museum in New Orleans, Louisiana. Interviews with Ehlers can be heard on the museum's website.

ARTHUR FREDERICK DEFRANZO (1919-1944)

Arthur F. DeFranzo enlisted in November 1940 in Massachusetts. In 1944, he was a staff sergeant in the 18th Infantry. On 10 June, near Vaubadon and the Cerisy forest, he was wounded whilst saving one of his men who had been hit by enemy fire. Despite his wounds, he led an attack against German positions and continued advancing and encouraging his men. He destroyed a machine-gun just before succumbing to his wounds. The body of Staff Sergeant A. DeFranzo was repatriated to the United States in December 1944 and he was buried with full military honors at Riverside cemetery in Saugus. Arthur Frederick DeFranzo was awarded the Medal of Honor for these heroic actions, on 4 January 1945.

ROBERT T. HENRY (1923-1944)

Robert Henry, from Greenville, Mississippi, was drafted in April 1943. On 3 December 1944,he was with the 16th Infantry. At Luchem (to the east of Aachen), several machine-gun nests were halting his platoon's advance. Private Henry threw off his helmet and wool overcoat, making himself as light as possible. He ran forward alone, armed with his rifle and grenades, across open terrain towards a line of bunkers. Hit by a burst halfway across, he picked himself up and continued advancing when he was wounded by a second burst. The enemy had been occupied with his actions and in the meantime his comrades had carried the position. Robert T. Henry was posthumously awarded the Medal of Honor on 12 June 1945. Henry, aged 21 when he died, was buried in his hometown. The American forces "Henry Kaserne" in Munich was named in his honor.

Robert T. Henry.

Top right, lieutenant Jimmie Monteith, Jr.

JIMMIE WATERS MONTEITH, Jr. (1917-1944)

Jimmie W. Monteith was born on 1 July 1917. He enlisted in October 1941 and was sent to Camp Croft in South Carolina for basic training. In February 1943 he was posted to the 30th Division at Camp Blanding, Florida. In April, he joined the 1st Division as a reinforcement officer and took part in the Sicily landings. In Normandy he was a platoon leader with Company L of the 16th Infantry, landing at Omaha Beach (Fox Red) where the fighting was particularly bloody. He was ordered to take a German strong-point (Wn 61). His Medal of Honor citation reads as follows:

"For conspicuous gallantry and intrepidity above and beyond the call of duty on 6 June, near Colleville-sur-Mer, France. 1st Lt. Monteith landed with the initial assault waves on the coast of France under heavy enemy fire. Without regard to his own personal safety he continually moved up and down the beach reorganizing men for further assault. He then led the assault over a narrow protective ledge and across the flat, exposed terrain to the comparative safety of a cliff. Retracing his steps across the field to the beach, he moved over to where 2 tanks were buttoned up and blind under violent enemy artillery and machine-gun fire. Completely exposed to the intense fire, 1st Lt. Monteith led the tanks on foot through a minefield and into firing positions. Under his direction several enemy positions were destroyed. He then rejoined his company and under his leadership his men captured an advantageous position on the hill. Supervising the defense of his newly won position against repeated vicious counterattacks, he continued to ignore his own personal safety, repeatedly crossing the 200 or 300 yards of open terrain under heavy fire to strengthen links in his defensive chain. When the enemy succeeded in completely surround-

Far right, Gino Merli.

Below, Francis McGraw.

Below, Jake Lindsey.

Staff Sergeant
George Peterson

ing 1st Lt. Monteith and his unit and while leading the fight out of the situation, 1st Lt. Monteith was killed by enemy fire. The courage, gallantry, and intrepid leadership displayed by 1st Lt. Monteith is worthy of emulation."

Jimmie M. Monteith lies in the American cemetery at Colleville-sur-Mer, Section I, row 20, grave 12.

GINO JOSEPH MERLI (1924-2002)

Gino J. Merli was born on 13 May 1924 in Scranton, Pennsylvania. He was drafted in July 1943 and was assigned to Company H of the 18th Infantry. At dawn of 4 September 1944, near Sars-la-Bruyère (south-west of Mons), his company was attacked by a larger German force. The position was overrun, but Private Merli remained with his machine-gun to cover his retreating comrades. When his position was overrun, he feigned death even when the Germans prodded the bodies with their bayonets. Once the German troops had moved away from his position, he got up and started firing again. On two occasions he fooled the enemy into thinking that he was no longer a threat, then attacked them again when they had left him for dead. For his heroism, Merli received the Medal of Honor from President Truman on 15 June 1945. For his actions during the Second World War, he received amongst others, two Purple Hearts and a Bronze Star. When he returned to civilian life, Merli worked at the Veterans Administration Medical Center in Plains Township, Pennsylvania. He returned to the Normandy beaches in 1984, accompanied by the journalist Tom Brokaw and was a source of inspiration for the latter's book, *The Greatest Generation.* He died in 2002.

FRANCIS XAVIER MCGRAW (1918-1944)

Francis X. McGraw was born on 29 April 1918 in Philadelphia, Pennsylvania. He joined the Army at Camden, New Jersey, and served in Company H, 26th Infantry. On 19 November 1944, his regiment was in the front-lines in the Hürtgen Forest. During the course of a counter-attack near Schevenhütte, Private McGraw held on to his machine-gun position despite intense fire and a lack of ammunition. Having run out of ammo, he picked up a carbine and engaged the enemy once more. He killed a German and wounded another in a desperate firefight before being mortally wounded by a sub machine-gun burst. He was awarded the Medal of Honor for these acts of bravery, on 25 October 1945. He lies in the American cemetery at Henri-Chapelle in Belgium. An Army troopship was named in his honor (1946-1952) as well as the McGraw Kaserne in Munich from 1945 to 1992.

JAKE WILLIAM LINDSEY (1921-1988)

Jake W. Lindsey was born on 1 May 1921 at Isney, Alabama. He enlisted in February 1940. On 16 November 1944, Lindsey was a Technical Sergeant with the 16th Infantry. On this day, near Hamich, his platoon was hit by a ferocious tank and infantry counter-attack. Despite being wounded, Lindsey fought hand-to-hand with a group of Germans and succeeded in holding the line despite intense fire, forcing two panzers to retreat. For these actions, he was awarded the Medal of Honor on 21 May 1945, exceptionally during a Congress session and from the hands of President Truman and General George C. Marshall. Lindsey went on to see action in Korea and left the Army with the rank of second lieutenant. Jake W. Lindsey died at the age of 67.

GEORGE PETERSON (.../1945)

Peterson enlisted in Brooklyn in 1941 and became a staff sergeant with Company K, 18th Infantry. On 30 March 1945, near Eisern, Germany, Peterson was seriously wounded in both legs by a mortar projectile. Despite the bleeding and the pain, he refused to withdraw and carried on fighting, succeeding single-handedly in knocking out three machine-gun nests. He was awarded with the Medal of Honor on 17 October 1945.

JOHN J. PINDER, Jr. (6 JUNE 1912-6 JUNE 1944)

John J. Pinder was born on 6 June 1912 in McKees Rocks, Pennsylvania. He enlisted in the Army in 1941 at Burgettstown and joined the 16th Infantry with the rank of Technician 5th Grade (T/5 specialist NCO). On 6 June, the 16th Infantry landed near Colleville-sur-Mer, under intense fire from the German troops. T/5 Pinder was carrying a radio and struggled to keep it above the water and reach the shore. His citation reads as follows: "For conspicuous gallantry and intrepidity above and beyond the call of duty on 6 June, near Colleville-sur-Mer, France. On D-day, Technician 5th Grade Pinder landed on the coast 100 yards off shore under

John J. Pinder, Jr.

devastating enemy machinegun and artillery fire which caused severe casualties among the boatload. Carrying a vitally important radio, he struggled towards shore in waist-deep water. Only a few yards from his craft he was hit by enemy fire and was gravely wounded. Technician 5th Grade Pinder never stopped. He made shore and delivered the radio. Refusing to take the cover afforded, or to accept medical attention for his wounds, Technician 5th Grade Pinder, though terribly weakened by loss of blood and in fierce pain, on three occasions went into the fire-swept surf to salvage communication equipment. He recovered many vital parts and equipment, including another workable radio. On the 3rd trip he was again hit, suffering machinegun bullet wounds in the legs. Still this valiant soldier would not stop for rest or medical attention. Remaining exposed to heavy enemy fire, growing steadily weaker, he aided in establishing the vital radio communication on the beach. While so engaged this dauntless soldier was hit for the third time and killed. The indomitable courage and personal bravery of Technician 5th Grade Pinder was a magnificent inspiration to the men with whom he served."

He was posthumously awarded the Medal of Honor seven months later on 4 January 1945. He lies at rest in Grandview Cemetery, Florence, Pennsylvania. The American barracks of Zindorf, Bavaria were named Pinder Barracks in his honor. They were demolished in 1999, but his name remains due to a town council decree at Pinder Park where one of the guard towers still remains.

James Reese.

JAMES WILLIAM "BILL" REESE (1920-1943)

James Reese, born in Chester (Pennsylvania) was drafted in November 1941 and served with the 26th Infantry. On 5 August 1943, in Sicily, during the fighting at Mt. Vassilio, Reese and his mortar squad held a defensive line during an enemy counter-attack. When their position was made untenable by enemy fire, he ordered the men of his team to withdraw and without any assistance, moved his mortar and began firing on the machine-gunners. With his last three shells, he managed to score a direct hit. His ammunition gone, he picked up a rifle and continued to advance to slow down the enemy, but after several exchanges of fire, he was mortally wounded. He was posthumously awarded the Medal of Honor on 17 December 1943. James Reese lies in the Chester cemetery, Pennsylvania.

After the Second World War, an American barracks in Augsburg was named Reese Kaserne in his honor.

JOSEPH EDWARD SCHAEFER (1918-1987)

Joseph E. Schaefer was born on 27 December 1918 in Queens, New York. He was drafted in January 1942 and became a staff sergeant with Company I, 18th Infantry. On 24 September 1944, near Stolberg, Germany, Staff Sergeant Schaefer and his platoon were holding defensive positions in the face of a German attack. Voluntarily putting himself at the most exposed part of the line, he brought down many attackers and single-handedly captured ten prisoners. On the same day, he took part in a counter-attack and succeeded in freeing a group of Americans who had earlier fallen into enemy hands. For his actions, he received the Medal of Honor on 22 August 1945. Schaefer went on to fight in the Korean War. He died on 16 March 1987 and lies at rest in the Long Island National Cemetery in Farmingdale, New York State.

Right, Master Sergeant Joseph Schaefer is awarded with the Medal of Honor by General Walter M. Robertson, commanding XV Corps.

ACKNOWLEDGMENTS

The authors wish to thank Nadège Lavit for her patience, Michel Pascal, the 'Duty First' reenactment group and Serge Balleux, as well as Jonathan Gawne, Morgan Gillard, Pierre Besnard (Le Poilu sarl Paris XV) and Yves Le Clair.

PHOTO CREDITS

NARA, 16th Infantry Regiment Association, First Division Museum at Cantigny, Michel Pascal, 26th Infantry Regiment Association, Real war photos, The First Division history, National WW2 Museum, Sophia Histoire & Collections photo archive

SOURCES

- 16th Infantry Regiment Association,
- First Division Museum at Cantigny,
- 26th Infantry Regiment Association,
- Lone sentry.com,
- The First Division history,
- 16th CT S-3 Combat Report,
- History 16th Combat Team Invasion of France
- National WW2 Museum.

BIBLIOGRAPHY

- *Danger forward, the Story of the First Division in WWII*, Society of the First Division, Washington DC, Albert Love Enterprises, 1947
- *Terrible Terry Allen, Combat general of WW2, the life of an American soldier*, Gerald Astor, Ballantine Books 2003
- *Beachhead Don*, Don Whitehead, Fordham University Press 2004
- *Spearheading D-Day, American Special Units in Normandy*, Jonathan Gawne, Histoire & Collections 2013
- *WW2 Order of Battle*, Shelby Stanton, Presidio Press
- *Omaha Beach*, Joseph Balkoski, Histoire & Collections 2014
- *Bitter Victory, the Battle for Sicily 1943*, Carlo d'Este, Harper Collins 1991
- *Clarence R. Huebner, an American Military Story of achievement*, Steven Flaig BA, Thesis prepared for the Degree of MA, University of North Texas 2006.
- *There's a war to be won*, Geoffrey Perrett, Ivy Books, New York 1991
- *An Army at dawn*, Rick Atkinson, Henry Holt 2003
- *Here is your war, the story of GI Joe*, Ernie Pyle, Henry Holt, NY 1943

H&C HISTOIRE & COLLECTIONS

Series Editor: Philippe Charbonnier
Translated from the French by Lawrence Brown and P. Charbonnier
Design and layout by Philippe Charbonnier

ISBN: 978-2-35250-464-1
Publisher's number: 35250

Published by
Sophia Histoire & Collections
5 avenue de la république, 75011 Paris-France
Tél: +33(0)1 40 21 18 20 - Fax: +33(0)1 47 00 51 11
www.histoireetcollections.com

Printed by Jomagar
in March 2017, Spain
European Union